HOW TO **Not Call** THE **Po'Lice** EVER

D1603239

VISIONED, LIVED & WRITTEN BY
**Tiny Gray-Garcia, Leroy F. Moore, Jr.,
Jeremy Miller, Joey Villarreal, Muteado Silencio,
Aunti Frances Moore & all POOR Magazine family**

A POOR Magazine / Prensa POBRE publication © 2020

ISBN: 9781732925076

Book design, and typesetting: A.S. Ikeda
Cover art: Asian Robles
Cover design: Stephanie Espinosa & A.S. Ikeda
Copy-editing & production team: Westyn Narvaez, Stephanie and Celia Espinosa, Michelle Kim, Yael Chanoff, Tiny Gray-Garcia, and Leroy F. Moore, Jr.

Mama Earth, Homefulness, POOR Magazine and Deecolonzie Academy Liberated Villages and all of our ancestors

You can get our books and online curriculum at
www.poormagazine.org
www.poorpress.net

A Note from the POOR Press Linguistic Liberation Team

As you read this beautiful POOR Press book, please understand that as colonized and oppressed peoples in poverty, we do not speak the colonizer's languages with academic precision. We resist linguistic domination by writing and speaking and creating. There will be typos and different uses of language. These are our voives, our art, and our resistance narratives. Read them with love and spirit in your hearts. Decolonize your mind one page at a time.

The photos in this book are of varying quality and size, and we chose to include them as they are. We believe this honors poverty skolas and the realities of poverty journalism. It was more important to preserve the photos as documentation rather than leave them out, and we believe the book is better because these images are included.

This book is dedicated to all the Suns and Daughters,
Mamas and Daddies, Auntis, Uncles, SisSTARS
and Brother Ancestors we have lost to Po'Lice
Terror and the lie of 911 calls in this stolen land.

Acknowledgments

Tiny Gray-Garcia

First to acknowledge and send love to Mama Earth, upon which we are blessed to even be existing, and ancestors of this part of Stolen Turtle Island—the Lisjan/Ohlone Nation (and their descendents, SisSTAR Corrina Gould, one of our powerFULL spirit elders at Homefulness and Elephant Council members), still here helping us all to liberate stolen Mama Earth after so much kkkolonial terror, violence and genocide.

To my Mama Dee, an OG poverty, ghetto skola, Afro-Boriken, Mixed Race, disabled, houseless, revolutionary single mama who had NO TIME for kkkops, Sheriffs, kkkorts, ICE, prison guards, parkkk rangers, school Po'Lice, their enablers, or any of the occupying armies ruling over this stolen land, but also had no time for violent, aggressive, hater, racist, classist, ableist, bullshit from any of us to any of us, and would tell you so immediately, whether you liked it or not. I miss you every day mama.

Love and so much respect to all our of fellow mama, aunti, uncle, grandmama, youth and elder and ancestor poverty, indigenous skolaz who have held and continue to hold all of our brokenness and re-healing in all of their collective hearts no matter how hard the Family Elders/Elephants Council meetings have gotten and will continue to get. Laure McElroy, Uncle Al Robles, Jean "Ish" Ishibashi, La Mesha Irizarry, Joseph Bolden, Corrina Gould, Fuifuilupe Niumeitolu, Diane Veilman, Bruce Allison, Kathy Galvez, Leroy F. Moore, Jr., Ingrid DeLeon, QueennandiXSheba, Jeremy Miller, Dee Allen, Israel Munoz, Xochi Maez Valdez, Sauda Burch, Katana Barnes, Brother Mink, Pearl Ubungen, Muteado Silencio, Juju Angeles, Jewnbug, Tony Robles, ViviT, Jason Fluker, Sue Ferrer,Joey Villarreal, Audrey CandyCorn, Mama Blue, Tracey Bell-Borden, Tiburcio, Amir, Ziair, Akil, Amun Ra, Kimo, Phillip Standing Bear, my Mama Dee Garcia and all of our mamas and so many more...

To the badass art of Asian Robles who creates images for all the pain we all experience and made the art for this cover and so many other covers still to come...

To Asa/A.S. who is one of the fiercest designers I have ever had the blessing of knowing who helped us all bring this beautiful book together.

To Westyn, Celia, Stephanie, Michelle Kim, Jasmine, Rae and Yael who helped the medicine of this book be manifested.

To Paige, Yael, Clemmy, Toby, Cynthia, Molly, Cecilia, Alex, Josh, Becca, Ellery, and so many more baaadass solidarity warriors who helped this even happen. Peter Menchini for his videography and photo stills.

Finally, endless revolutionary love to all of the poverty, indigenous skolaz, Black, Brown, houseless, poor, Mama, Daddies, Uncles, Auntis, Daughters, Suns and Trans family who have died behind the lie of Occupying armies, who NEVER have kept us safe, and the thousands of powerFULL warriors for justice and truth all across this stolen land and beyond who refuse to give up, give in or look away, NO MATTER WHAT....

Contents

Prayer

Corrina Gould, *Chochenyo/Karkin Ohlone*

Grandmothers and grandfathers, creators, and ancestors, we thank you for this day and for our lives. We thank you for giving us the ability to be here with one another in this circle. We ask grandmothers and grandfathers to watch over us and the work that we're doing, to open our ears, and our minds and our souls to lead in a better future for the next seven generations and beyond.

We pray for our grandmothers and grandfathers, for all of those that are on the front lines. That are standing up against all of the isms. That are standing up for sacred sites, for our relatives that are behind the walls and on the borders, and that are in prison through things that are unjust. We asked grandmothers and grandfathers for special blessings, for those that are living without a home right now, for those that are in fear, for those that are having difficulties right now. We pray for all those that are sick right now, and all of those that are worried right now. For our relatives that are passing over into the next world.

We pray for them and those that are left behind. We ask grandmothers and grandfathers to help us to weave together the work that we're supposed to do on this earth right now. So that we can survive, so that we can have good water and air and good soil for the next seven generations and beyond. That we create the beauty that we want to see in this world. That we do not put that on the next generation, but that we rise up together to make this the real thing, the things that we want. We ask grandmothers and grandfathers to bless all of us and the work that we're doing and help us to spread the work to all over the world. Oh oh oh....

Stop Calling— (the Po'Lice)

Tiny Gray-Garcia

Stop Calling
Stop Stalling
Stop Talking while more Black and Brown Daughters and Suns are
    fallen
No I mean Stop enabling and Kolonizing
a system that kills
more than it ever cures our ills
with roots in the original theft of Turtle Island
Meant to CONfuse our already CONfused mind-Sets

Got us all believing that numbers like 911 mean housed people are
    safe from us houseless—
that WitesAndLites are safe in their own embedded desire for
    wealth-hoarding wite-ness

that continuing to buy & evict, foreclose, sweep, and kick—
makes anyone safe from myths
About how to be safe
and what is the way to handle fear and danger everyday
In a place already stolen
A land already rife with murderous lies that keep getting told and
    sold
Like poison

That Was set up to Shoot and Kill every Black, Brown or poor
    person in their way
Was locked in to support fear
so more protected classes could steal
And more of us could end up in their jail cells making them more
    blood-stained dollar bills

These are the legacies of the Stealing Fathers And the Kop-callers
And the way to unlink the Po'Lice from Po'
Is for you to stop and think…

Why am I callin—
And how did I EVER believe safety meant
Dialin
9-!-!

—Tiny, 2020

Foreword

Rae Leiner & Jasmine Syedullah / Vassar College & Hudson Valley for Black Lives (aka Akkkademia infiltrators)

Because intersectionality and the movement for Black Lives is a thing (a liberation thing), it's important. When we're calling for Black Lives, we're calling for all Black Lives! That includes women and femmes, that includes people who are differently abled and neurodivergent. That includes children and elders. That includes queer folks, trans folks, anybody on the LGBTQ spectrum. All Black lives matter, right? Just wanted to raise up and make visible that piece about intersectionality. When we're talking about the work of dismantling systems of oppression, but we can't recognize how to dismantle white supremacy within ourselves, we can fail. We can end up creating community security and it can look just like the police in policing liberation. Our liberations are bound together, no matter what, right? In order for the "opposition" to use the argument that "all lives matter," all lives can't matter if Black Lives don't matter, right? We recognize that, and we recognize that there are communities that we're connected to that have amazing strategies for how to handle issues of safety and security.

—Rae Leiner

Policing is not just a profession—it's a prerogative, and it's a prerogative that has infected all of our social lives, our sense of safety and expectations of security in our neighborhoods. In order to abolish it, in order to defund it, we have to see how it's moving through our communities and relationships with and across spaces of affinity and difference. We have to notice how it shapes our reactions to harm, how we police, survey, patrol, punish, and cancel people we share community with. When we begin to think outside the very, very tight cage of its hold on our imagination of safety we can shift the focus towards each other and what we each need to feel safe in real time. To be more accountable to each other—that's what Homefulness has really raised up. That there are people working and building community accountability together completely beyond the reach of this gross infrastructure of the police and they are surviving and thriving, it is proof-positive that we all can survive without the police.

It's going to be important for us with access, wealth, and privilege to learn from those who have the most direct experience with the police, poverty, and disenfranchisement. What accountability and public safety without reliance on the police can look like. It's going to take a whole lot of collaboration, particularly with folks that a lot of us living with with access, wealth, and privilege don't generally have contact with, or accountability to. We don't often turn to the folks who are most marginalized, the most policed, the most incarcerated, for lessons and to learn on how to do this work of dismantling power. They are exactly the people who have the key to our collective future, they are working in the future and we would like to catch up with them.

—Jasmine Syedullah

Co-Introduction

Some of the powerFULL POOR Magazine/Homefulness/
DeeColonize Academy Family

Welcome to the *How to Not Call the Po'Lice Ever* handbook. This is presented by the POOR Magazine Homefulness family of very poor, houseless/formerly houseless, disabled and indigenous Poverty Scholars. This book and this work is rooted in what we at POOR Magazine call Poverty Scholarship—which means a combination of prayer, poetry, theater, love, song, rhythm and talk-story. I am Aunti Frances, elder poverty skola, founder of Self-Help Hunger Program, co-founder of Homefulness and a Black Panther….. *and I am…. that Black Woman that I am….who's celebrating my deliverance, liberation and freedom from the broken chains of lies and deceit.*

—Aunti Frances Moore

I'm Tiny—That Houseless mama—that houseless daughter—all the people you don't want to be, don't want to see, look away from me… what you gonna do—arrest me…im in your citeee? I Rock my jailhouse

Attire cuz me and my po mama did jail-time for the "poverty kkkrime" of being unhoused in this occupied indigenous holla........

The medicine we are presenting in this humble handbook is meant to help everyone who reads this unfuck their minds from the amerikkklan prescription for "safety." This is not a magic bullet. It might not work for everyone, and really is grounded in the values of inter-dependence rather than what I call the continued and violent "cult of independence," which this stolen indigenous territory was built on and promoted/demanded by the "Stealing Fathers" (so-called Founding Fathers) and all of the other violent bloody paper trails that worked to steal Turtle Island from the 1st Peoples of this land.

We at POOR Magazine are all peoples coming from severe trauma of Po'Lice terror, criminalization, houselessness, disability, eviction, incarceration, false borders and more, so we live and walk this talk as both survival and desperation. We walk, live and teach this to you and each other so hopefully more of our Black, Brown, Disabled and poor babies aren't killed, devastated by Po'Lice terror. And in addition, so we won't kill each other, because as folks coming from trauma, we hurt each other all the time...in addition to poverty skolaz/survivors of trauma and Po'Lice terror, we are also Po' poets and cultural workers. We teach, walk and speak through poetry, prayer, verse, spirit and cultura...because there's more than one way to transform, heal and build out of 527 years of aristo-kkkrazy , genocide and death...

—Tiny Gray-Garcia

My name is Muteado Silencio, *My words are my bullets. My pain is my gun. So sit back and relax because we going to drive by your minds.....* POOR Magazine is a poor people led, indigenous people led, multi-ethnic, multi-generational... We are people who have come out of poverty, out of being homeless. Some of us are angry, myself being persecuted by these ICE customs, immigration customs. Again, as you see in this beautiful photo, this is a village of mamas, aunties, daddies, uncles, black and brown folks, still struggling through poverty, disability and healing. With that said, just to be real too, that we as folks of color coming from poverty had never seen the police, or these

institutions as friends. They incarcerate us and put us in jails, and claim to be an institution "to protect and serve."

—Muteado Silencio

I'm the Black, Sexy, fly cripple. Look at me. Look at me. Hear this. Hear this. I'm Jim Crow, I'm Porgy, I'm Harriet Tubman. Yes, I'm here, we're here and we will always be here...

I'm Leroy Moore, Black, Disabled, Poverty Skola in residence with POOR Magazine, co-founder of Homefulness and founder of Krip Hop Nation and the information we are sharing with you is not a national movement. It's not a hashtag, it's not a Ford Foundation grant. It is community building one community at a time. It's a different way of giving, sharing what our community needs, not what the police needs. That means we rely on community building from the inside out. It's not community policing. It's just community...

—Leroy F. Moore, Jr.

I'm JV, Chicano warrior, working with the Republic of Aztlan Chicano-Mexicano Resistance, because we understand that in order to uproot systems of oppression like white supremacy and US imperialism, we have to obtain national liberation. Without it, we will never overcome these systems of oppression. Working with my POOR Magazine familia, fighting for the people. Joey Villarreal: Author, Artist, Media producer of FreeAztlan Radio on PNN-KEXU Po' Peoples Radio at Homefulness and survivor of the Plantation Prison Nation known as the SHU (Secured Housing Unit at Pelican Bay)...

—Joey Villarreal

Fragment 2017

No non-profit organiser
Can speak for the poor.
No college professor
Can speak for the poor.
I can speak for the poor because
I'm still among the poor.
Count my head among the broke on this block
You'll see me.
'Cause I own less than you,
You'll dis me—
These slums—mine
Frustration—mine
This thirst—mine
Starvation—mine
These wants—mine
These tears—mine
Displacement fears—mine
They're with me all the time
No president is mine
And neither is his government
They straight represent
The class hate I resent
I don't count
To institutions in power

I don't count
To a racist coward
Picture me not once
Worshipping their flag
As long as they continue
To deny & slag—
No news reporter
Can speak for the poor.
No social worker
Can speak for the poor.
I can speak for the poor because
I'm still among the poor.
Count my head among the broke on this block
You'll see me.

—Dee Allen, Poet, Author, Co-builder/poverty skola, land liberator and formerly houseless resident of Homefulness... This slam bio/poem is available in *Skeletal Black: Poems From Beneath The Poverty Line,* POOR Press, 2019.

Chapter 1
Herstory

Original art by Joey Villarreal created in the SHU "torture cell" at
Pelican Bay and from the book *Aztlan Realism* by Aztlan Press

Anthropology, Ethnography, Psychology

The Study About Us Without Us...

Tiny Gray-Garcia

The notion of poverty scholarship was born in the calles, prisons, street corners, community centers, welfare offices, shelters, kitchen tables, assembly lines, tenements, favelas, projects, and ghettos— all the places people don't look for educators, experts, leaders, researchers, lecturers, linguists, artists, creative thinkers, writers, and media producers.

Poverty scholars are told our knowledge is not valid or legitimate. Our speech is improper; our work and our choices, criminal; our words, inept.

Poverty scholars like us are usually silenced: incarcerated, criminalized, displaced, homeless, disabled, marginalized, sorted, separated, and extinguished.

Poverty skolaz' schools are everywhere. Our teachings are essential, haphazard and immediate, fluid and static. We are your mama, your cousin, your elders, your corner-store owner, and your recycler. Our research is based on our lives and our experiences, our solutions, our vast knowledge of what works and what can work. Our visions are based on the dreams of our ancestors, our elders, and our youth...

Excerpt From *Poverty Scholarship: Poor People-led
Theory, Art, Words and Tears Across Mama Earth*
published by POOR Press (**www.poorpress.net**)

Another Naked, Disabled Black man being tortured by the Po'Lice-from a list by Leroy F. Moore, Jr. of "Naked Black and Brown men Killed by Po'Lice" on **poormagazine.org**

Historical Sketches on Policing

Jeremy Miller

Policing has always been about the reproduction of social order through violence. This said, the often referenced "monopoly of violence," contrary to popular belief, does not belong to the police per se, but actually belongs to those who pay for them. Originally this funding came from the "princes," you know—kings, queens, emperors and the like, but at this point they have been replaced by corporations and banks. What about taxes and the concept of civil-service (police as civil servants) one might ask? Well yes, we do pay their salary with our tax dollars, but (even under a "Defund" scenario) we are not in control of this expenditure. To put it a different way, all banks make money by gambling with our money. This is and has been the setup. Any bank that is halfway "healthy" (incidentally "public health" has long been considered a police matter) is full of both money and graft. People have never appreciated being economically exploited, and thus if your entire raison d'etre is to exploit people, you can anticipate people contemplating counter-violence unto you. From a European standpoint this could be rendered as the Robin Hood or Jacobin effect. From an African standpoint the Maroon would be a reference here. For protection of your avarice, you want people with sticks and if they have "fire-sticks" all the better. This is the origin of policing. The innovation then was to convince the people that protecting those who were robbing them was in their own interest. The basic argument (which is very impolite to distill down) winds up sounding like a refrain from a Cosa Nostra tape: "You know when I break your legs for not paying me on time, it helps you out, because you can't run away from paying me as easily, and if you hadn't run away from paying me your legs wouldn't be broken, so really you should be paying me for breaking your legs." Which, incidentally, is exactly what we do not only through tax-payer funded police salaries, but also through tax-payer funded settlements in those rare cases where successful litigation is brought in response to police atrocity. They kick our asses and then we (not them) are collectively responsible for "making each other whole again."

PARIS

The first real manifestation of an organized uniformed police force dates back to 1667, and was instituted by Louis XIV for the "management" of Paris. Their job definition laid bare the true purpose of policing and has, despite variations, remained remarkably consistent for the last 353 years. Their job was, "ensuring the peace and quiet of the public and of private individuals, purging the city of what may cause disturbances, procuring abundance, and having each and everyone live according to their station and their duties."

The "peace and quiet of the public and private individuals" was always in reference to the elite classes. Poor and working people were not considered to be individuals, for they were only valued insofar as their labor could be exploited. They were the *sans culottes* or the "toiling masses" that Marx and his acolytes would reference a couple centuries later. "Purging the city of what may cause disturbances" was a dual reference to broke and homeless people, and also to revolutionists. As a minor theme it also dealt with a handful of "crimes" as they are commonly understood today but that was the minor, not the major premise. "Procuring abundance" is as clear as it sounds: extort the poor and guard the robber barons' and royalty's ill-gotten gains. "Having each and everyone live according to their station and their duties"

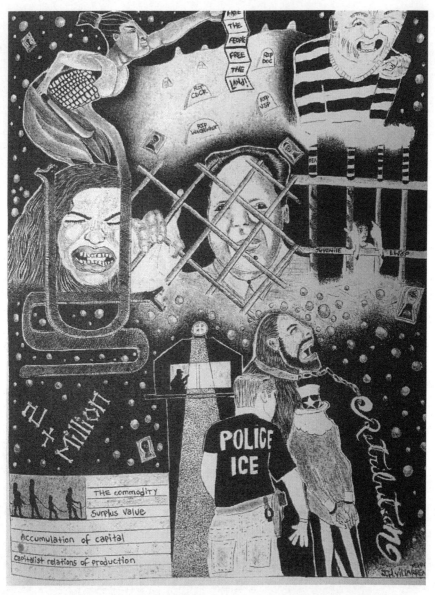

Original art by Joey Villarreal created in the SHU "torture cell" at
Pelican Bay and from the book *Aztlan Realism* by Aztlan Press

means quite simply, "Shut the fuck up peasant. Don't even think about
questioning your oppressor!" Sound familiar?

MILITIAS

Approximately 50-odd years earlier in what would eventually become the United Capitalist Prison States of America, a different strand of policing would begin with the compulsory militia movement. This was created by European colonizers for two purposes. First, it served to insulate the "governors" from the violence of other European men who often lived on meagre resources (women and others were not contemplated in this power dynamic) similar to the way Wahhabism and its derivatives insulate the Saudis from the roughly 10 ½ million men they don't share wealth with, by sending them on jihad against the "infidel" defined by the rulers as whoever is the convenient target of the moment (again women and immigrants don't count!) Second, all of their colonial towns and territories were directly stolen from the indigenous inhabitants of this land and thus they required protection to: a) steal more land and property (often achieved through murder and genocide,) and b) protect against indigenous folk that might "steal it back!" Sister Roxanne Dubar-Ortiz does a great job writing about this strand of policing history.

BACK TO EUROPE

At the end of the 18th century, right around the time that the French were warring with the British, the French became more explicit reverting from the term police which implies some sort of civility, to the term *gendarme* (gens d'armes) which can literally be translated to armed men. Following this the British, led by Sir Robert Peel, (the reason London cops are still called "Bobbies") in order to distinguish their coercive urban management from the French in the first quarter of the 19th century, decided that a more polite approach was necessary. In nine principles set out in the "General Instructions" for London's Metropolitan Police in 1829, the counterintelligence form of policing (euphemistically rendered as "modern policing") was born. The first two "principles" illustrate this well:

To prevent crime and disorder, as an alternative to their repression by military force and severity of legal punishment.

To recognise always that the power of the police to fulfill their functions and duties is dependent on public approval of their existence,

Original Art by WRAP (Western Regional Advocacy Project—**wraphome.org**

actions and behaviour, and on their ability to secure and maintain public respect.

Thus in order to enhance the *power* of police to achieve despotic goals traditionally obtained coercively by military force, the respect of the public must be *secured*! Remember the Cosa Nostra example above, "It's for your own good!"

Armed Guards lined up at San Quentin Prison Main gate to meet peaceful protestors of continued mass incarceration in COVID-19 epidemic

SLAVE CATCHERS

There is a theory floating around that the first cops were slave catchers. It is true that slave catchers were around as early as the 16th century, especially in the Carribean, but these were largely volunteers and/or "owners." The real heyday of slave catching comes after the ratification of the Fugitive Slave Act in 1850, which required all citizens and local law enforcement to aid in the capture of runaway slaves. This is why it enters our history here, as it expands on the respectability politics of "modern policing" to compel the actual participation of the general

public in the coercion. As such, it doubles as one of the origins of policing, and also an origin of cop-calling/vigilantism. It is important here to note the economic aspect of affairs. Despite a natural emphasis on the racial aspect of chattel slavery, people tend to forget that chattel means property. Let's not get caught up in the class vs. race debate. In the United Capitalist Prison States of America there is no coherent way to effectively separate the two since the classes were formed based on racial identification/subjugation and thus to minimize either aspect results in an incomplete analysis.

UGLY LAWS

Assaults on poor and disabled people (often co-incidental with one another, and in the eyes of "law enforcement" often treated as indistinguishable) have long been a part of policing. Remember the imperative from Paris to "purge the city of what may cause disturbances." A spectacularly ugly manifestation of this phenomenon originated in San Francisco in 1867. This was the first "Ugly Law" in the United Capitalist Prison States of America. Ugly Laws were a series of ordinances that explicitly criminalized poverty and disability. San Francisco's original ordinance focused specifically on the "unsightliness" of begging. Again, what makes this noteworthy in our history of policing is not the aggression towards poor and disabled people which had been ongoing for centuries already, but the creation of actual laws to codify this specific targeting for regular enforcement by the police.

PHILIPPINES

In 1901, French scientist Paul-Jean Coulier developed a method to transfer latent fingerprints on surfaces to paper using iodine fuming. This greatly increased the usefulness of the fingerprint identification that had just recently begun to be used in crime solving a few years earlier in Great Britain and India. That same year the United Capitalist Prison States of America commenced its colonial governance of the Philippines under William Howard Taft, later to be the 27th President of the United Capitalist Prison States of America and also 10th Chief Justice of the US Supreme Court. Needless to say, many Filipin@s were not feeling the colonial regime and so in order to prevent uprisings, the new regime beta tested some of the most modern techniques of coercive policing in the Philippines. This protection of the colony imperative led to the earliest widespread use of fingerprinting, and also one of the earliest systems for keeping criminal files/profiles on people complete with photos and fingerprints. After a successful colonial run, much like Taft, these methods were then exported to the United Capitalist Prison States.

MODERN PERIOD, POLICE BRUTALITY, AND REFORM

My goal in writing this brief historical sketch on the origins of policing must end here. To address all of the changes that occurred during the 20th century, which is when we see prohibition, Jim Crow, convict leasing, growth of mass incarceration, the war on drugs, SWAT, school resource officers etc., is beyond what I can fit in this brief survey. The purpose of this exercise was to uncover some of the early origins of policing and not just for masturbatory historicity, but to address a political point having to do with the twin discourses of "police brutality" and reform. Quite often as our gaze turns to policing and its attendant abuses, we are faced with this phrase "police brutality" but to quote David Correia and Tyler Wall from their brilliant book, *Police A Field Guide*:

[Hence] referring to police violence as a form of brutality is at once an identification of police with an animalistic quality, an uncivilized, bestial violence. The irony here is that the police institution has historically framed itself as the supreme instantiation of civilization. Historically, the term civilization was once synonymous with police—to police is to civilize, to polish or make polite (note the etymological links with police) the uncivilized and impolite brutes threatening white bourgeois order.

I concur with Correia and Wall's analysis here, and hope that my historical sketch helps illustrate this fallacy. This is important because the distinction is not devoid of active political content. As Correia and Wall continue:

What commonly goes by police brutality works to demarcate between acceptable and unacceptable state violence, and therefore simultaneously works to legitimate all sorts of police violence that might not be deemed excessive or illegal.

Point being, police are violent. It is an essential feature. And this has always been a violence that carried racial, patriarchal, and most omnipresently class aspects and implications. When we speak of police brutality we are yet again implicitly co-signing on the presumed existence of a fictitious, legitimate, non-violent policing. Sir Robert Peel

JUSTICIA PARA
LUIS GONGORA PAT

HONOR MAYA

would be proud. Unfortunately this is the same thing as co-signing on our own oppression. This leads to the closely related fallacy of police reform. Policing is a coercive assault on the life and liberty of anyone that is not of the ruling race/class/gender/sexual orientation, there is no such thing as a reform that truly helps us. To quote slain Freedom Fighter George Jackson:

We will never have a complete definition of fascism, because it is in constant motion, showing a new face to fit any particular set of problems that arise to threaten the predominance of the traditionalist, capitalist ruling class. But if one were forced for the sake of clarity to define it in a word simple enough for all to understand, that word would be "reform."

Our liberation is intimately tied with our ability to love and care for each other. It is also intimately tied to abolition of the agents of our oppression. If we don't fall for the reform Okey Doke, and push for actual self-determination of our own security and affairs, perhaps the next historical sketch can be of the 350 years and holding history of liberation that we helped inaugurate. Food for Thought. All Power to the People.

UGLY LAWS

Making it Illegal to be Houseless & Disabled in Public

Leroy F. Moore, Jr.

> *We see the history of police and the history of people*
> *with disabilities, and the history of people that are*
> *poor linked together...* —Leroy F. Moore, Jr.

The Ugly Laws are the codes and lies (laws) we're living under today. For those of you who don't know the names of them in your city, rest assured you have them. Literally hundreds of laws on the books that are present day versions of ancient settler, colonial lies. I mean, laws. I call them lies or lie-gislations that make it illegal to be poor in public i.e, laws that say its a citable offense to walk, stand, sit, sleep, park, convene, or be alive while houseless in the not-ever public, public domain. That the engagement with the Po'Lice currently is not only is the 21st century lynching program and 21st century white supremacist terror program but the Anti-poor, anti-disabled peoples program, that has reigned terror against houseless, poor, disabled bodies for centuries.

202

Original art by Joey Villarreal created in the SHU "torture cell" at
Pelican Bay and from the book *Aztlan Realism* by Aztlan Press

Chapter 2

Po'Lice Terror of Our Poor Bodies

Original art by Joey Villarreal created in the SHU "torture cell" at
Pelican Bay and from the book *Aztlan Realism* by Aztlan Press

Houselessness & KKKop-Calling

Tiny Gray-Garcia

> *"It's definitely been said that there are two different trucks.*
> *One that things that are of value get placed in and one that*
> *garbage gets placed in. Or sometimes they'll just throw it*
> *all together. We're supposed to be able to claim our stuff 90*
> *days after CalTrans and Po'Lice come. I know people who*
> *have had their stuff not been there. And I know people who*
> *have watched their stuff get put in trash compactors."*

> —Reena, houseless poverty skola, reporter from
> RoofLESSRadio on POOR Magazine talking about
> the weekly and violent CalTrans Sweeps of houseless
> peoples belongings that happen across California.

Hygienic metaphors and poverty

> *We need to clean up that blight...We need*
> *to clean up that neighborhood...*

> —Politrickster from AnyCity, United Snakkkes...

We have all been krapitalized into the starbuxization of our landscape—in other words, led to believe that the absence from an environment of people, specifically poor, houseless, disabled people somehow means it's "clean". This is especially ironic considering that in this krapitalist society there is no guaranteed housing or shelter, which means that many of us will absolutely end up outside in the cardboard motels like me and mama used to live in, but if our bodies and belongings are automatically illegalized, this means we are only guaranteed two things, to be murdered by police or incarcerated for our poverty.

It is and always has been the way that poverty is dealt with in this Stolen land. It's really important for folks to understand and overstand that these benign sounding laws that are constantly being passed in your cities and towns are different names for the same settler-kolonial

Image of "Aunti" Frances Moore and Momi Palabraz of the Self-Help Hunger Program and POOR Magazine, along with POOR Magazine family in front of a "porta Pottie" we made for the politrickster that continued to call the Po'Lice and DPW on the Self-Help Hunger Program's Porta Pottie.

laws that make it illegal to be houseless in public. From Sundown Towns to Stop-and-Frisk, these laws also enable and cause the ongoing Po'Lice terror, killing and profiling of poor/houseless/disabled/POC peoples to even be in neighborhoods where for many racist, classist, ableist reasons the "residents" who "own" Mama Earth have decided you don't belong. We know that this entire stolen land project (United Snakes) has been originally created to support the wealth hoarders and land Stealers.

One of the most important roles for Po'Lice is to keep in place the lie of buying and selling mama Earth as a commodity, i.e, to protect the false krapitalist notion of "private property" ownership, "income property" and the entire real eSnakke industry which is one of the reasons for the rampant calling the Po'lice on folks for just living, being, standing while Black, Brown, or houseless. People like Luis Demetrio Gongora Pat, murdered by Po'Lice from a call by a genttriFUKer neighbor for the "crime" of being houseless, indigenous and brown in public. Or Steven Taylor for being houseless and Black and having a mental health crisis in public.

Then similarly, which is equally as terrifying, you have laws on the books that make it illegal to be a young person of color in public convening (Gang enhancements). Then you have other industries built and behind the warehousing that we know as the plantation prisons. But what about the elder ghettos? What about the endless and intense multimillion dollar foster care industry? The child separation services (Child Protective Services), all of these came from the original settler, settlement houses and what I call the anti-social work industry, which are all rooted in hetero-patriarchal white male notions of normalcy and similarly, safety. As well, rooted in our absence, as homeless peoples, from your landscape. The fact that we and our belongings are now subject to what I call the *"violence of exposure"* i.e., being seen in the public domain because we don't have access to a roof. And even more dangerous if our public domain is in proximity the endlessly stolen acres and acres, miles and miles, blocks and blocks of "private property".

Locally in California and other cities that are filled with the gentry-tech nation and newly gentri-FUKed hoods and barrios, there is an actual attack on poor people for our mere presence and ongoing series of Po'Lice calls against our exposed belongings and bodies.

These kinds of Po'Lice calls on the public land (that isnt really for all of the "public") are the ones that plague our sister warrior and co-founder of Homefulness and founder of the Self-help Hunger Program, Auntie Frances Moore, who literally had to fight the city and the gentri-fucking neighbors, because the porta potty and hand-washing station they acquired at Driver Plaza, in North Oakland, is and was being constantly criminalized. Driver Plaza, which is the site of the Self-Help Hunger Program, is a beautiful tiny park which is a space for gathering of houseless and low-income Black elders of North Oakland, many of whom were displaced by the same kkkop-calling gentrifukers out of that very neighborhood. As Aunti Frances often says: "Public Land is for Public Good", but sadly we see over and over again that so-called "Public" (read stolen indigenous territory) land is never meant for the poorest of the public. And these notions of who belongs in certain places are what undergirds the use, abuse and system of genocide perpetrated by the police on poor peoples bodies and lives.

Example of "Violent Architecture" as described by Lisa Ganser/PNN

Leroy F. Moore, Jr., Lisa Ganser (PNNWashington) Mama Dee and me as well as other warriors at POOR Magazine, WRAP, and the Coalition on Homelessness, have lifted up and worked to resist, dismantle and absolish for years because poor, disabled, houseless

Original Art from WRAP-Western Regional Advocacy Project

peoples of all ages and elders can't sit in public while poor, disabled and houseless. Benches and stoops and doorways and window sills are spiked with violent architecture and/or just removed because as poor folks, we don't have the right to rest.

The Violence of Exposure Versus the Privilege of Privacy means that because you have access to a roof no one is able to "judge" your messiness, disorganized room, hoarder/clutterer tendencies, depression or substance use. Those of us living outside are constantly judged, criminalized, Po'Liced, murdered and incarcerated for things you housed people do everyday without even thinking about what someone else would think about you for doing them.

The Cult of Rehabilitation—If housed people have a mental health crises', become enraged, severely depressed or get absolutely fuked up on a substance, it is only if they have a witness or family, that the Po'Lice are called. If you want to be alone, hide-out, self-segregate, no-one will judge you or force their low-key cult-of rehabilitation, savior industrial complex/helping industry demands on you.

Whereas, if you are houseless and outside, every moment of your life is in the public domain, and people either criminalize you or impose their "helping" on you even if you haven't asked for it. This is why I ask people as they un-link their minds from the Po'Lice they realEYEz that even their heart-felt "help" is an act of privilege and often, violence. It can, in the case of Luis Gongora Pat and so many others who were killed by a "help" call or "well-check" end up in our deaths.

Hoarder/Cluttering Versus Archiving and Collecting: The Privilege of Privacy

One of the lessons I always give as a poverty scholar is, imagine someone took the roof off of your room or apartment, would they call you messy? Would they call you dirty? Would they call you a hoarder clutterer? And how is it that Bill Gates and Jeff Bezos and other wealth-hoarders/land stealers all across Mama Earth can hoard several billion dollars, multiple vehicles, several residences, condominiums and "vacation homes" when they only need one to live in, drive in and/or keep their families housed. For all this hoarding they will be called "collectors, "archivists" successful, wealthy, or rich. Conversely, if we houseless and poor, traumatized peoples have too many cardboard boxes, newspapers or bicycle parts we are pathologized/criminalized/labeled "hoarder clutterers" and subject to belonging theft/seizure, the violence of "sweeps" and arrest.

> *Anti-Social Workers and Case Manglers Call me*
> *Crazy , Lazy, Dumb and a bum, cause my knowledge*
> *don't come from the instituSHUN...*

—Tiny

Shout Out to SisSTAR Susan Schweik, author of the powerful book *Ugly Laws*.

Original art from WRAP-Western Regional Advocacy Project

Kkkop-Calling on Culture, Color & the Lie of Safety

Leroy F. Moore, Jr. and Tiny Gray-Garcia

(Partial Transcript of the Racist kkkop-called fueled arrest of Mali Watkins of Alameda, CalifAztlan, aka Klanameda)

PO'LICE: Hey man. You look like you're having fun. Everything okay?

MALI: I'm getting my exercise. I live across the street. Is there a problem?

PO'LICE: Okay. Someone called us because you were dancing in the street and they were concerned for your safety.

MALI: So I'm dancing near the street?

PO'LICE: It looked like you were dancing. I was watching you for a little bit. It's like Jazzercise type of thing?

MALI: Exercising.

POLICE: Is there any particular reason you're not doing it on the sidewalk?

MALI: Because people walk on the sidewalk and I jog sometimes, I move a lot.

PO'LICE: I just had a couple more questions man. And then we'll be on our way. Just want to make sure where you're at. Do you feel like hurting yourself today?

MALI: Have a good day gentleman. Have a good day gentleman.

PO'LICE: Listen. At this point, you're detained. You understand? You're not free to go. You're not free to go. You're not free to go. Put him over in the street. If you resist, you will be put under arrest....

Excerpt from the horrible Po'Lice terror waged on Mali Watkins of Alameda, because of the violence of kkkop-calling on Black and Brown men, women and trans communities in this stolen land.

What Does the Community Need?

Leroy F. Moore, Jr.

It's hard to go on once you "hear" the aforementioned Po'Lice terror. The question is, where are we now? We are still at a point that a lot of people are talking about working for the police, police commission, all of it toward the police, focused on what the police need. But we say, turn the focus to what the community needs.

What the community needs has never been the police, not clean policing, or community policing, or trained policing. I bring up the example of Mario Woods. His mother was seeking mental health services before he was shot by Po'Lice but mental health services are few and far between for poor people.

So, that's what we need. We need more services in our community. So, when you talk about abolishing the police, we also need to talk about the transition period. So, when the police is gone, we need to have a lot of money coming to the community. And what that means is, is that this society needs to learn how to lead a transition period, learn how to re-educate our community of not calling 911. Listening, learning how to rely on each other like we do at Homefulness, like we are teaching in this book, like Tiny teaches on in PeopleSkool and Poverty Scholarship about interdependence...

Poor/Houseless/Migrant/Indigenous land liberators & prayer-bringers/spirit carriers from POOR Magazine un-selling another small part of Mama Earth on BlackArthur in Deep East Huchuin (Oakland) for the creation of Homefulness #2

Land Liberation Must Be Embedded with Po'Lice Abolition

Tiny Gray-Garcia

As we discuss liberation from the Po'Lice we must talk about land liberation and the end of what I call "the lie of rent". The murders of Luis Gongora Pat, Amilcar Perez Lopez, Jessica Nelson Williams, Steven Taylor, Margret Mitchell and so many more houseless Po'Lice murder victims can all be traced to their homelessness, gentrification and displacement. In addition, the deaths of Shannon Marie Bigley, Desiree Quintero and Papa Bear, can all be traced to police, sheriffs, park rangers and private security guard harassments, terror, negligent homicide and murder because of their homelessness (see articles in Po'Lice stories section of this book) As we houseless and formerly houseless, disabled Black, Brown and indigenous revolutionaries discuss and live Po'Lice abolition, the conversation is ALWAYS

Armed Po'Lice conducting a violent "sweep" at "Stockton Blvd. Camp" in Sacramento. Credit: Sacramento Homeless Union

embedded with a conversation about land liberation. People should clearly understand and overstand that one of the reasons we poor folks at POOR magazine are able to live into this vision and practice this medicine we are sharing in this book, is that we are actively living, working and educating our youth and elders at a homeless peoples solution to homelessness we call Homefulness.

Homefulness is a self-determined landless peoples movement that is spiritually and legally unselling a small piece of mama earth in deep east Huchuin-Ohlone Land, aka Oakland, on BlackArthur Blvd.

That's why us Po'Lice terror victims can even manifest this curriculum and this book. Houseless mamas like myself and Frances who don't have a pot to piss in and a place to call our own, would not be housed right now, because the pandemic called poverty has been going on way longer than the pandemic called COVID-19. The pandemic called police terror and its relationship to poverty is Absolutely entwined with our access to land. And that land access is absolutely tied to our collective safety and security without the Po'Lice state.

So as Luis Demetrio Gongora Pat was not only killed for being a Mayan indigenous man in racist Amerikkklan, he was killed because he was a houseless Mayan, indigenous man who had been illegally evicted from his San Francisco apartment and then murdered by the aforementioned violence of exposure in gentri-fuck-cation city aka

Aunti Frances Moore, Tiny and other poverty skolaz from POOR Magazine's Stolen Land Tour of SF Tech in a tent in the lobby of SalesForce Building, which displaced over 120 disabled, unhoused San Francisco residents to build more gentryTechNation offices

San Francisco, i.e., not because of a 911 call, but because, like brother Mali Watkins, someone was "worried" about him and dialed 311—a non-emergency help line that although not the Po'Lice, engages with the Po'Lice. The cult of the Karens, or what I would call the cult of the Caring's. The cult of rehabilitation, the savior industrial complex at its most deadly example is more common than people know.

And then to take the Po'Lice predation of houseless bodies further, we must speak on Shannon Marie Bigly and Desiree Quintero, both killed by the violence of "sweeps". In Shannon's case, killed because Killtrans (Caltrans) has been conducting "sweeps" on houseless peoples for years who hide on the side freeways and roadsides. In this case, Shannon was picked up and thrown in the trash while she was sleeping in a cardboard box. So, these are all connected. And what they are connected to at their core, is *land*. How can we be police-free and pol-lie-free if we have no access to places to sleep safely or have the "right to rest" as our comrades at WRAP call it.

It is not just about not calling 911, it is also about teaching and unteaching the lie of wealth hoarding, land stealing, un-packing the soft ambivalence of "owning classes" and trust-funders and surplus income-holders into manifestation or what I call transforming blood-stained dollars into Love-stained dollars for liberation.

There is no more time for talking, philanthro-pimping, grant-dancing, ruling class ass-kissing, politricking, studying, lie-gislating, or gentriFUking. And if anybody reading this has a trust fund, contact this povertyskola and/or consider urgently enrolling in PeopleSkool. I say urgent because wealth hoarding itself and the way people are taught to hoard resources and land is a sickness that is absolutely at the core of many of these phone calls to police. That is just one of the many pol-lies.

Homefulness Was Built With A Story...

—Tiny

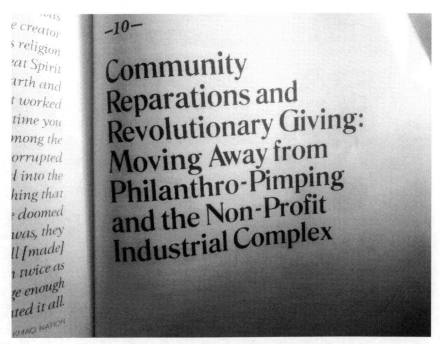

Cover page of Chapter 11 from *Poverty Scholarship: Poor People-led Theory, Art, Words and Tears Across Mama Earth)*

There's no money in the bank.

POOR

Videography & stills by Peter Menchini

"Where's My Money Bitch??"

Theatre of the POOR/Teatro de los Pobres—TheatreLearning on How to Not Call Po'Lice in the Workplace

Below is an excerpt of the transcript of the Theatre of the POOR production. Created for the *Not Calling the Kkkops in the Workplace* training, (which we do whenever and wherever we are invited in). The theatre was based on an incident which happened at POOR Magazine's humble shared/squatted office space in the Mission District of San Francisco, the request for kkkops to be called was made by another tenant in the office, a non-profit organization which works on immigration justice in the global South, but is not part of the POOR Magazine family.

Narrator, Poverty, Disability Skola Laure McElroy introducing the Theatre of the POOR Scene

Because we at POOR Magazine believe that people like us, who are in poverty and in struggle, need to be paid for our time. Because anytime that's taken out for activism, creativity or communication, is possibly one less loaf of bread that we could have gotten from a hustle, work, struggle to survive. And that because all of us poverty skola writers are in poverty, it is that much more important to compensate for our time, words, and scholarship. POOR Magazine is in fack Po as Tiny often says, so the money that we use to compensate this media work is from our subscribers, radical redistributors, come unity Reparators and supporters.

This is hard also as we are always fundraising and teaching and helping people unlearn the lie of hoarding but we keep doing it because we live in a capitalist, blood-stained dollar economy and money is real and charged with a lot of bullshit. We work really hard to decide and operate the circle and all the things we do, and all of us agree from the perspective of poverty scholarship that people should get paid.

Similarly, because we are all poverty skolaz in different states of struggle with substance use, homelessness, incarceration, trauma, mental health crises and more we also can lose track of our own blood-stained dollaz and then turn on each other, cause we the closest to each other. On this day, one of our longtime members showed up under the influence of several substances. It was a highly explosive situation.

RAY: Hey Tiny! Tiny! Tiny

TINY: What? What's up, fam?

RAY: What's up man?

RAY: Where my money at? Where is my money at? I didn't get... (HOLDS UP HAND) Uh-uh, no tricks. No fast talking me. Uh-uh. Where my money at?

TINY: I don't have any money. Remember They gave you the cheque last week. Remember?

RAY: Hell, no.

TINY: Yes they did—we were all there...

RAY: I didn't get no cheque.

TINY: Yeah, yeah, yeah, yeah, yeah.

RAY: Tiny, give me my damn money.

TINY: I don't have it. I don't have it. I don't have your money or any money, you know that.

RAY: Bitch, you going to give me my damn money—

MUTEADO ENTERS THE SCENE

MUTEADO: What's going on guys?

RAY: You've got my money, Tiny.

LEROY ENTERS THE SCENE

LEROY: Come on. Come on, man. Come on.

RAY: What? Wait, well write me a cheque out now.

LEROY: Come on.

TINY: There's no money in our bank account, you know that too.

RAY: No, no, no. I need it now.

LILY (NEIGHBORING NON-PROFIT ORG STAFF PERSON ENTERS SCENE)

LILY: Somebody call the cops. Call the cops. Call the cops.

RAY: No, no, no. Don't call the cops. No, no, no, no, no.

LILY: Call the cops. He's out of control.

RAY: No, no, no, no, no. No. Where is my money?

LILY: You need to call the cops.

RAY: No, no. I didn't get no... Don't—

BRUCE (ELDER, DISABILITY SKOLA) ENTERS THE SCENE

BRUCE: Hey, you want to fight me? You want some of this? You want some of this?

TINY TO BRUCE: Back up. Back up.

BRUCE: We can go right now. You want some of this?

RAY: Tiny, Tiny. Let me talk to Tiny. It's between me and Tiny. Come here Tiny. Come here Tiny. Come here Tiny.

BRUCE: Leave her alone. Your fight's with me.

LEROY: No, no, no, no. No violence.

MUTEADO: Hey, you know what? You're drunk. You're obviously under the influence.

RAY: No, I'm not.

MUTEADO: You should not be here where you're under the influence. You know that man. Come on now.

LILY: What are you guys waiting for? This is a workplace—we are working on social justice—call the cops now.

TINY: Ray... listen bruh (LOWERING VOICE, CONSPIRATORIALY) these other fools gonna do something stupid—you know we got u bruh—come back tomorrow, when you're not under no shit, and we'll figure it out. Come back tomorrow, and when you're not under no shit, we'll make something happen.

MUTEADO: Okay. Chill. Chill.

RAY: Don't call the police.

LEROY: Just come back tomorrow mang.

MUTEADO: Just come back—you know we got you....

POOR MAGAZINE FAMILY CIRCLES RAY

RAY: Tiny? Tiny, Mute, Leroy? Can you give me a couple of dollars? Just give me a couple of dollars.

TINY: We've got you, bro. I've got you. I got you.

RAY: Can you give me a couple of dollars? And then tomorrow.

LEROY: Come back tomorrow.

BRUCE: Go home.

LEROY: Come back tomorrow.

RAY: Okay.

TINY: You've got to breathe there. You're going to make it.

LEROY: Come back tomorrow.

RAY: All right. All right.

MUTEADO: You're not yourself.

RAY: Ok—see you tomorrow.

RAY EXITS THE STAGE, PLAY CLOSES

Being "Too Loud" and Other Classist HypoKrazeez

Tiny Gray-Garcia

"Where's My Money Bitch??", is just one example of *Not Calling the Po'Lice Ever in the Workplace*—where we are surrounded by so-called conscious "woke" "revolutionaries" who might work, paid or un-paid in the non-profiteer industrial complex and yet operate in the very systems that their "mission statements" and values fight against. Working on global south and local militarization, oppression, homelessness, tenants rights, racial justice, poverty and Palestine and then calling the Po'Lice on poor, Black, Brown, Houseless, in-struggle people on this stolen land.

There was another famous Po'Lice call example that this poverty skola spoke up about and then was forever blacklisted for doing so and silenced from speaking in that media channel forever. That case involved an "angry Black woman" media volunteer whose voice was "too loud" in the non-profit media workplace as she was taking care of her business on a public phone on her lunch break, their response after she refused to leave was to call the Po'Lice. The non-profit media agency works on covering social justice issues locally and globally and yet couldn't "see" that calling the killer kkkops on a single Black low-income mama in their workplace was the same kind of oppression they were dedicated to "reporting" on. I call this hypokkkrazy and it happens all the time.

And for us survivors of the hypoKrazy, "*Where's My Money Bitch??*" was exemplary of the constant ways we as poor peoples hurt each other, take care of each other and resist the constant, endless demand by everyone to call the Po'Lice on us—even people that are "woke" or conscious or know better.

The Private sekkkurity industrial complex is another crucial aspect of the genocidal workplace story, leading to so many folks being profiled for shopping, working and walking while Black, Brown or houseless. Racheted up to the 21st century sci fi dynamic we see the installation of the robot kkkops/surveillance cameras employed by wealth-hoarding tech companies in San Francisco to "accompany" employees to their cars, and troll the parking lots so the delicate gentryTechNation doesn't have to "deal" with unhoused people asking them for change, or if any unhoused people do ask tech employees for change, they will be harassed by the robot kkkops. This and other colonial crimes of the Tech industry is why us houseless, displaced poor peoples created the TechReparationsFund of the Bank of ComeUnity Reparations, a fund to build/create Black/Brown working class San Francisco/Oakland residents equity who had suffered eviction/displacement, foreclosure and other gentrification-fueled removal in the last 5-10 years since Tech colonized the Bay Area.

For us as poor, trauma-filled and hurting poverty skolaz, this is not a Winnie the Pooh in the sunset hippie utopia. There are so many struggles, so many ways we are constantly pushed, threatened, triggered, terrified, violated and betrayed, by each other.

Stop picking the leaves off these bushes, dude.
My family lived here way before you did. Way before you did.

Videography & stills by Peter Menchini

"This is My Land…"

Theatre of the POOR/Teatro de los pobres
TheatreLearning on Landless peoples Movements
challenges and resistance of the Po'Lice State

BOB: This is my land. My land. I used to live right here. This is my food. I'm going to pick my food. This here is my land.

LEROY: Yeah, my land.

LEROY: This is my land. I live here.

MUTEADO: Please don't take all of the plant—just leave the roots at least—our youth at the school planted those—

LEROY: Some? This is my land. I live here. I live here.

NEIGHBOR: He doesn't seem that safe. What do you think?

BOB TO MUTEADO: Fuck you and Gentrification bullshit. This is my land.

MUTEADO: I know man, but the kids actually worked on this garden. And a lot of them aren't ready to pick—

BOB: My family lived here way before you did.

DEE: Stop picking the leaves off these bushes, dude.

MUTEADO: Just leave some for the other folks.

BOB: It's my land. I played here. I used to live here.

DEE (ANOTHER FORMERLY HOUSELESS BLACK RESIDENT OF HOMEFULNESS): This is no more your land than it is my land. Everybody shares this land in common.

BOB: What are you? Uncle Tom? My land.

MUTEADO TO DEE AND OTHER POOR FAM: Careful guys. Careful because he got really violent last time.

NEIGHBOR: Are you guys sure I shouldn't call the cops?

DEE: Keep them out of this. We'll handle this.

TINY TO BOB: Hey, I want some weed too. Can you leave me a little bit?

BOB: What? Who are you, man?

TINY: Just take some of it bro. Take some of it. Take some of it. Let me get you a bag though. I'll get you a bag. Okay? I'll get you a bag and then you can come back tomorrow and get more if you want?

BOB: I can come back tomorrow?

TINY: Yeah, of course. Of course.

BOB: And the next day?

TINY: Of course. It's your land.

BOB: And next year?

TINY: It's your land. And we need to report to you on how it's going too. So, we need your scholarship here—Just leave a little bit of it for us. That's all. Just leave a little bit.

BOB: A little? Just a little? All right. Yeah.

TINY: All right.

MUTEADO: Just don't destroy the garden man.

BOB: I'll be back tomorrow.

TINY: Okay.

BOB: Same time.

"This is My Land" is a reenactment of our experience at Homefulness, a landless, homeless, self-determined movement. This scenario was based on our experience with Bob, an unhoused African man whose family used to own property on Blackarthur comes to Homefulness' in deep east Huchuin (Deep east Oakland). He was angry from years of systematic racism and forced removal behind fake paper trails, slave contracts and colonizer laws, coded under titles like Blight and Taxes. Bob comes on to homefulness land where his family used to own property before they lost it to a tax bill and threatens violence, pulls up the truly poor people, led all Pachamama Po' peoples garden that feeds the whole neighborhood and was launched, grown, created by youth and elders in poverty from BlackArthur—including all the tomato plants, orange trees, basil and chamomile, and then when the plants were gone, proceeded to steal the hay that feeds our therapy goats. When community asks him to stop he says this is my land, this is my weed, and threatens violence and other acts against all of us houseless and formerly houseless folks of homefulness.

Postscript: We offered Bob an apartment, space, home, and even bench of his own to sit on, or hay bale (weed) of his own, he wanted none of it—deciding instead to act as a "supervisor" of his land, who would take his "weed" when and if he wanted it. In many ways, Bob demanded, acquired, Garvey-ite self-determined, reparations in a way that only he would dictate. His own ongoing revolutionary moves, un-accountable to anyone else as hard as it is/was is the medicine of Liberated land in all its complicated, beautiful, difficult and real manifestations...

—Tiny Gray-Garcia

Poor Peoples Security & Autonomy

Muteado Silencio

I also want to add that many of our folks resort to physical violence. In *This is my Land*, the brother actually pulled out a knife in one incident and in at least three other times screamed at us and raised a hand to threaten violence, which among other incidents prompted our family elders councils and our elephant councils to assign folks from within our village, within our community who would act as a *Poor Peoples Security Teams*. So, when situations like these go down, there are some people who are better than others at diffusing a situation instead of adding more gasoline to the fire.

As you notice too, that when shit goes down like this, we all come together as a unit to back each other up, and help to bring each other to an innovatively more peaceful place, even if it means getting inside their story and respecting their story. In a lot of these incidents, our family members show up intoxicated and then get really violent and when it was just one or two people facing off, they will continue to act aggressively, but as soon as they see there was three or four people, it also tends to diffuse the aggressiveness... And again, in the case of *"Wheres My Money Bitch??"*, even though Ray was drunk, he wasn't stupid. And slowly he desescalated the situation without us even involving anyone but us. We've been doing this for the last 20 years. It ain't easy. It gets scary. Sometimes you feel your own safety in danger. But as a community, we stand with each other and we're there in the good times and bad times...

Kkkorts & revolutionary movement infiltration

Tiny Gray-Garcia

Another system we don't mess with is the kkkorts. More specifically, eviction kort and Juvenile dependency kort. Which when all of us houseless folks launched homefulness we were sadly tested in a way that almost dismantled everything our ancestors, elders, youth and all of us worked so hard to manifest.

In the very first beautiful year of Homefulness, we offered one of the original homes of the first three units we built from the ground up with reparations, blood, sweat and so many tears over the summer of 2013 to homeless and/or very low-income families. A single parent moved in who looked like us, talked like us and claimed to have the same values, dreams and hopes as us.

Sadly this person had an agenda that made us all think she was working for the State, as we did nothing but be who we always were, moving with love, support and liberation. But within 6 months of residing at Homefulness, this person seemed to be intent on destroying the reputation and good name of POOR Magazine and many of our individual collective members, with on-line slander and attacks, lies about our children and elders and then refused to leave, pay their contribution to the overall costs that we ask of everyone who lives here or do some kind of poor people sweat equity, (anything from writing to teaching to care-giving) which is the other option. And instead, they literally inhabited one of the largest homes on Homefulness for a year and half filled with rage, lies and destruction.

Many of our long-time members were triggered to "get legal" with them, serve them with eviction papers, etc, and eventually felt so harmed by this persons attacks on all of us that many long-time POOR family left the organization, because they felt like we should do more to get "rid" of their extremely harmful spirit.

But as hard as it was, we never wavered, we stood by our manifesto for change, never changed our tactics, or pursued kkkorts or legal means. As emotionally and spiritually violent and painful as it became and dragged on, we continued to work through a process of endless and painful mediation. In addition to multiple Elephant and Family

Council Meetings, where this person was verbally abusive to our elders and refused to respect the process (that they had helped to write in their early days of their residence in a document called The Peoples Agreement), we eventually called in an outside mediator to hold a year long process and create an agreement, which they also didn't respect, but eventually left after they found another residence (sadly, this persons trauma is/was so great and so dangerous that they ended up doing the exact same thing to the next person they moved with, who eventually reached out to us for help)

This sad and sorrowful story isn't the only time all of our values, principles and hearts were tested, again as poor, colonized people tragically we assault, fragment,abuse and inflict emotional and physical harm on each other all the time and similarly, we hold each other all the time through the hurt to the best of our ability.

One of the lessons learned in this traumatic time and others with folks in so much struggle with trauma and colonization, was the fact that we all have been conditioned into the cult of immediacy, which similar to the cult of rehabilitation and independence, makes us believe that we need to solve, fix, resolve, end, terminate issues, problems, struggles and crises' "right-away" which becomes a rationale for calling 911, the Po'Lice, the anti-social workers—someone, anyone, who can resolve our problems. Even if it means someone dies.

Sometimes patience in and of itself is liberation.

Patience and a recognition that not everything can be or has to be resolved at all and that sometimes, waiting, praying, sleeping, dreaming, contemplating, mentoring, traveling, walking, breathing and time itself, can bring us all into another place with a conflict, fight, struggle, crisis, etc. And as I say this, I overstand that if your very life is in danger, you can't slow down or have patience, and that every situation is distinctly different and in no WAY are we making one size fits all statements about everyone and every situation.

Abolishing The Other Po'Lice—
The Mandated Reporter

Tiny Gray-Garcia

> *We don't engage with Any agency that tests,*
> *arrests, incarcerates or leads to our deaths...*
>
> —*Tiny*

In addition to Po'Lice, Sheriffs, park rangers, school Po'Lice, housing Po'Lice, private security guards and Kkkorts, we as poor and traumatized peoples do not engage with Child Protective Services (CPS), Adult Protective Services (APS), Truant Officers or other "officers" of the state, ostensibly put in place to control and supposedly protect the most vulnerable among us (see article in Po'Lice stories chapter).

For us as poor people/land liberators, this is especially complicated because we run a liberation school for children in poverty and care-give for multiple elders and families in poverty, and are actively building a different way to live and be in a society that does not support us. This means that we refuse to engage in the concept of Mandated Reporter, which is what our positions dictate.

See full story on the violence of mandated reporting in Chapter 4.

From the Occupied Land Truth Tour by Tiny.
Image Courtesy *El Paso Times.*

FAMILY COUNCIL, ELEPHANTS COUNCILS, ELDERS' Councils & ALL The Circles

Tiny Gray-Garcia

(In addition to PeopleSkool's poverty journalism, poor press poetry, writing and radio workshops for poverty skolaz and degentriFUKation seminars for folks with Race, Class and Formal Education Privilege.) We have several circles at POOR Magazine/Homefulness and Decolonize Academy which is how we decide all of our decisions, resolve and deal with conflicts and hold all of us fellow poor peoples in accountability and love. No matter how hard it gets... All of the below listed circles begin in a good way with all-nations prayer.

The Elephant Council

Elephant Council is so named because, like Elephants, we poor and traumatized folks are interdependently connected to each other, like

POOR Magazine/Homefulnes Elephant and Family Council Circles

Elephants, who no matter how hard a white zoologist might work to keep alive in "captivity", an elephant cannot survive without their family. And like Elephants we are matriarchal—mama and daughters, sisters and Aunties and Grandmamaz lead our core values, while we work with, listen to, respect and rely heavily on our Uncles and Suns, Fathers and Brothers.

In the Elephant Council, all of us are leaders and this is the ONLY way we decide things. We call our main decision making body which is led by poverty, disability, indigenous skolaz—the elephant circle—as we move like our elephant relatives—interdependently—ALWAYS down to think thru and continue to work on and vision this poor and indigenous peoples led movement.

ComeUnity Newsroom Circle/ComeUnity Orientation Meeting

Once A Month, for the whole ComeUnity to learn, share, create community news and get support for actions and create their own media and advocacy.

Post-COVID, Socially Distant, Outside ComeUnity
Newsroom/Comeunity Orientation Circle

POOR Magazine/Homefulnes Elephant and Family Council Circles

Revolutionary Building Circle

We hold our Revolutionary Building Circle to Deal with all building decisions between "papered" builders, so-called architects, engineers (who donate their time as part of their ComeUnity Reparatons), alongside community indigenous builders and poverty skola builder-leaders at Homefulness. We deal with the settler colonizer papers, requirements, struggles and permit gangsters who we intentionally navigate so this poor peoples movement will never be stolen from us poor people by the multiple settler colonial lies (laws) put in place to steal poor and indigenous people's land, lives, and equity.

Healing from Addiction thru Art, Liberation and Spirit (HEAALS) Circle

Extremely important circle, held every other week to help us trauma-filled poor peoples who have sought out the mans poison (alcohol, substances) to numb, self-medicate and survive another day of poverty in amerikkkka. Holding each other through healing and love and

Youth and Family Council for DeeColonize Academy Youth Poverty Skolaz

hope and change thru spirit, art, meditation and talk-story from all four corners.

Hoarder/Clutterer Trauma Support Circle

For Homefulness residents held bi-weekly to deal with our traumatized souls very real ways of coping thru collecting.

Family Council for Youth at Deecolonize Academy and Family Council for Adults at POOR Magazine

Similarly, if we have serious breaches of our Rules of Respect, in either our youth/children school community or our adult community, the Elephant Council calls a Family Council—this is another circle of eldership, healing and accountability.

FAMILY ELDERS Council

Our last and ultimate circle is called when things cannot be resolved in the other circles and to make final decisions that are permanent.

Homefulness—a homeless peoples, self-determined
solution currently in construction in the Sunset

These are held as both healing medicine and resolutions to decide where and what we should do as per our peoples agreement and can sometime lead to asking people to permanently or temporarily step away, for long periods of time or forever.

All of our teaching so far brings us to overstand and understand the value and moves of our multi-nationed indigenous ancestors from all four corners who worked in different ways together to solve, resolve

Asks Agreements with love of your POOR family while in class, circles, and radio sessions:
- Under/OverStand that these respect rules are rooted in LOVE - the only way we can all do what we trying to do- is by loving, respecting and listening to each other
-No Cross Talk- when someone is talking- pls don't interrupt or talk over them - One Microphone
- Please raise your hand to speak
-Please no aggressive, violent behavior to one another- try to refrain from hand gestures - or finger pointing
-If these things happen- All members are asked to stand up and stop the mtg- DO Not Try to keep the mtg going when behavior is escalating between members
-No Name calling - refer to the rules of respect by youth skolaz-
-Please be sober
-Practice healing/calming/breathing exercises with yourself before you come into circles/classes/ community spaces
-If you start to feel agitated or upset - its ok to step out of mtg

-If the facilitator notices any member getting agitated or angry they will ask that member to step out and breathe and sit with them until they are feeling lighter- or calmer- or if they are unable to calm down once they step outside the facilitator will assist that family member in leaving the mtg and arranging a different mtg time

- this is the Only way we can continue to operate a no PoLice calls landless peoples movement- this is rooted in love and respect - more than anything else for each other

each others problems, who also shouldn't be fetishized, as though there weren't flaws, but had nothing to do with this krapitalist, hoarding culture.

Controlled by the wite-hetero-patriarchal cult of independence, the ways in which people are forcibly (read: voluntarily) separated into what I call the separation nation, beginning with age-grade separated schools progressing to the cult of angst and then "voluntarily" traveling to cities and towns and states hundreds and thousands of miles away to age grade separated schools and colleges-and all of this is considered success. The ways that we are encouraged/almost forced to leave culturally and societally away from all of the things that we or our ancestors came from, our collective systems of protection, love and actual security, our origin stories, ancestors, families homes, communities. Until we end up struggling with isolation, fear, aloneness, make unsafe choices, have no elders to assist us, school us, protect us. (Disclaimer: narrative doesn't apply to people targeted, abused, tortured by their families. This is some of the de-gentriFUKing and un-colonizing work we do at PeopleSkool presented by POOR Magazine poverty skolaz and some of the many issues we address in the book: *Poverty Scholarship: Poor People-led Theory, Art, Words and Tears Across Mama Earth.*

These sad realities of colonial domination and krapitalist CONfusion have led us as houseless/indigenous/landless poor peoples in diaspora from all four corners and from this land has led us to create several circles of healing, decision-making, accountability and comeUnity justice at POOR Magazine. The Elephant Council is held in place and dictated by our Rules of Respect. When someone breaks from the rules of respect we also call upon another circle. (see above)

Our Rules of Respect or Peoples Agreements are fluid documents that are subject to change and growth all the time based on the changing, fluctuation of the Homefulness residents, POOR Magazine family, Deecolonzie Academy student body and other projects' needs. Because again there are macro and micro ways we re-traumatize each other as colonized peoples trying to organize each other and build a different, healing space. What you saw in the vignettes were really obvious ways, but sometimes they're literally much smaller and very internal. So we had to make these very fluid documents from the beginning rooted in love. And that's a very important aspect to any folks who are thinking about some of these models for themselves and their communities. If you make a series of agreements with each other, don't make them be static, because things Always change, communities change and crises can change. And as well, you never quite know what triggers people's trauma until you end up with a trigger. So you, again, can have these beautiful sessions where you come up with agreements all day and twice on Sundays, and they may mean nothing in practice.

A complicated example of this is we had a conflict in an Elephant Council where one of our beautiful poverty scholar members literally flipped off and cussed out another member. Which led us to realize that the rules of respect document we were working with was absolutely not comprehensive enough for our new larger family and extended family of houseless and homefulness resident poverty skolas.

Resisting Krapitalist Productivity Violence

Tiny Gray-Garcia

And then we had to recognize that we really, in an inner circle, still as traumatized people, had to come up with a more comprehensive model of de-escalation, because we're all going to escalate. Because we are all one feeling away from hyphy escalation at all times, cause you don't go through lives and struggles and false fucking borders and out of the violent incarceration Nation and come out just okay.

And in addition to de-escalation tactics itself, we also had to deal with really holding people's pain, even in the agreements themselves, letting people know that we felt the pain and we actually had space for it. And then at the end of the day, if we didn't get that decision made, well then who fucking cares? Maybe we'd spend the whole meeting just making somebody feel better or closing down the meeting because that day was just too hard. And again remembering our collective patience is really important as well—pain over krapitalist "productivity."

21 Years of Liberation Work

Leroy F. Moore, Jr.

These circles are the result of 21 years of work by POOR Magazine. This prayer and love-work and liberation accountability doesn't come overnight. That's why I talk about a transition period for people because it's a slow process. It needs to happen one inch at a time like we have and are manifesting at Homefulness.

When we do our How to Not Call Po'Lice workshops, our people ask, "Well, what about murder and what about rape?" Yes, those are very serious things and we have actually dealt with very serious issues regarding our communities in Family Councils and we also understand that many of us aren't there and that might be a reason where you have to make that call to Po'Lice if you are in that situation, but the reality is almost 70% of calls made are well-checks, and racist, classist suspicion and mental health crises. You don't need Po'Lice for a medical crisis, we don't need calls for most of the things that we call police for.

The Revolution Will Not Be Melted In A Pot

Tiny Gray-Garcia

One of our lived values is a saying i repeat often "the revolution cannot be melted in a pot." We all honor the different places that we walk to spirit. We all honor, whether we walk to spirit through a colonized church, through white Jesus, as my sister Nandi calls it, or through prayer to Mama Earth, as many of us do. Those are all beautiful walks and there's no one or right or wrong way. But one of the important aspects is honoring people's distinct and different directions of prayer, honoring people's culture, where they come from and how they move, that we're not a melting pot, that we're very clear that we're a very multigenerational, multiracial, multicultural, and multilingual movement. That's how you build a poor people's movement. That Race and Class and Disability and Gender and Culture are very serious aspects of people's trauma and healing and all of these things must be held and loved and lifted up.

Which brings us to one of our hardest, saddest, gut-wrenching and yet real resolutions/decisions of all, which was taught to me by multiple elders, including my Mama Dee, sometimes you need to ask people to step away forever. It's a very difficult thing. It is something we very, very rarely have done, but let's also not get caught in this eutopic notion about, why can't we just all get along? That's not real either. And again, what we're talking about is real shit. This is truth medicine. Sometimes the act is so egregious, the violence so severe or recurring or the conflict so impossible to resolve that we have no choice.

This is also understanding and overstanding, that we've been lied to and that our problems are solved through pharmaceuticals, the Western therapeutic industrial complex, or the cult of independence. Which bring us to the example of the Peoples Agreement that we say took us over 527 years to build, 22 years (of POOR Magazine life) to pray, and 11 years (of Homefulness life) to write.

Here is an excerpt:

Peoples Agreement for Homefulness Residents

1 I, _____ understand that this herstoric document heretofore known as *The Peoples Agreement* is rooted in the 525 year struggle of all of the co-founders, residents and future residents who are landless, indigenous, houseless, poor and criminalized peoples who have suffered wite-supremacy, forced diaspora, chattel slavery, border hate,different forms of abuse,violence, removal, gentrification, racism, hatred, incarceration, profiling and/or multiple forms of systems/institutional abuse in this stolen indigenous land the colonizers call the US.

2 I understand that this, *The Peoples Agreement*, is a sacred document, not held together by armed agents of the state (Po'Lice, Military, etc) but by each other, poor folks, working together, self-determined, with humility, and love.

3 I understand that by signing it, by agreeing to live here on the sacred land we call Homefulness, you are making a commitment to your fellow human, animal and land, to follow the rules of respect stated here, as well as the agreements listed below.

4 I understand that this document is grounded in the Declaration of Inter-dependence created in 2009 at the Revolutionary Change Session and the Manifesto for Change created by Mama Dee & Tiny in 1996 along with Volume 1 of POOR Magazine entitled Homefulness—a poor people-led solution to Houselessness

5 I understand that I/we are stewards of the land—we, the landless, indigenous, poor peoples who live/work/ learn on the land at Homefulness & our children & our childrens children and generations beyond—DO NOT OWN MAMA EARTH. None of us who live here/work here/learn here/heal here "own" the land, but because this land and all of us exist within a capitalist system who will easily take a certain amount of blood-stained dollars to evict us, displace us or remove us—we understand that their needs to be some entity on paper that "owns" the land or it will get stolen by more government gangsters or devil-opers.

POOR Magazine/Homefulness Family at Oakland Shitty (City)
Hall action against permit gangsters in January 2020

For that reason we are creating a series of spiritual and legal
documents and entities to protect the land and its stewards
from current or future removal, devil-opment or removal.....

—Excerpt from the Sacred "Peoples Agreement" created
by Homefulness dwellers, residents and founder youth,
adults, elders and ancestor poverty/indigenous skolaz.

The above is an excerpt of a poor people-created liberation "MamaFesto" it goes on to talk about how we're going to spiritually and legally unsell this small piece of Mama Earth and so much more that we all hold ourselves to on this sacred land.

None of this UnSelling and liberating by us poor and houseless folks would be possible without the "Buying" of Mama Earth first with Blood-stained dollars transformed into "Love-Stained Dollars". And because we poor folks/poverty skolaz have no access to blood-stained dollars, that would not be possible without the radical redistribution of folks with race, class and/or formal education privilege who read and follow the Poverty Scholarship Textbook, attend PeopleSkool sessions and/or become founder-funders of the Bank of ComeUnity Reparations and the POOR Magazine Solidarity Family.

We are releasing a Homefulness Handbook in 2021 to share with all other poor and indigenous people-led movements so they can replicate the Homefulness model which was always created as a healing model for mama Earth and her earth peoples in this time of so much krapitalist harm and extreme poverty and homelessness. We also go into corporations, organizations and institutions like Vassar at the invitation of radical liberation teachers like Jasmine and Ray (who did the foreword of this book) and share this medicinal model for MamaEarth.

And after realizing that even land trusts were a settler colonizal lie, that all have an expiration date we have begun the process to create a new legal distinction called the Liberation of Land Trust.

Finally, as you can see, there are so many different layers that hold us, weave us, heal us together to act as alternatives to the State. Because if you're actually trying to move off Po'Lice state terror then you have

POOR Magazine/Homefulness Family at site of Homefulness #2
on the first in a series of Prayer and Land Cleaning Days

to build/construct/create ComeUnity Liberation. The hard part of course, is that those of us who are poverty scholars in leadership here are also overworked and never paid and struggling ourselves. So it's a lot of work to actually hold each other, not only to this sacred land liberation commitment but to community love and respect, which then transforms into ComeUnity Security/ community support and life-long liberation from a system that tests, arrests, incarcerates and leads to the death of every poor person it gets.

> *This is the time that we can do/embrace/learn what POOR Magazine's been doing for 21 years. This is not the time to attach yourself to the democratic party, it's time for radical change and liberation, and we can do this right now.*

> —Leroy F. Moore, Jr.

Original art by Joey Villarreal created in the SHU "torture cell" at
Pelican Bay and from the book *Aztlan Realism* by Aztlan Press

Chapter 3
Building an Elephant Council

Original art by Ottis Smith

ComeUnity Newsroom & POOR Magazine/Homefulnes
Elephant and Family Council Circles

Family Elders

In order of eldership

Elephant Council and Why to Not Call 911 Ever   The reason why I am on the Elephant Council of Poor Magazine is that my only child, Idriss Stelley, was killed by SFPD when he was 23 in San Francisco. He was shot 48 times. It was supposedly a psychiatric intervention and he had no gun. So, right away there was a meeting at the quaker's building and Poor Magazine staff was there. Not only, you know, there were a lot of people that came there, for political reasons. But it was clear to me that the staff and friends of Poor Magazine were there, with their hearts, you know, with an integrity, with—they were authentic. So I knew, right away, that I could trust them, and immediately loved them.

Soon enough I started writing in Poor Magazine and becoming a part of their extended family. As I aged, and became disabled, I was part of the Elephant Council. Where we sought—whenever there's a conflict, within or outside of the organization, and—we seek resolution

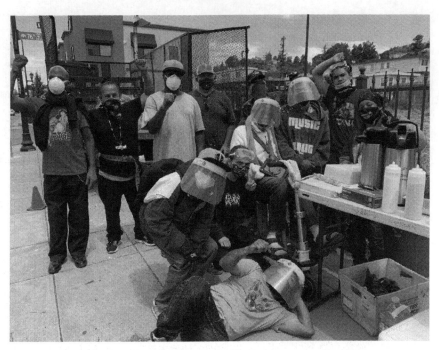

POOR Magazine/Homefulness Family at site of Homefulness #2
on the first in a series of Prayer and Land Cleaning Days

together, rather than to call the authorities. The "authorities" would be—the Po'Lice or any type of security or law enforcement.

For the past four years the Council has been instrumental in creating and implementing a training for the community that is about—NOT TO CALL the Po'Lice. We actually create different scenarios that are very common at street level or in a home, where typically people would be calling the Po'Lice for "help." Because we are acculturated to think that the Po'Lice are your friend, when we soon find out that the Po'Lice kill the person that was alive, you know?

Calling the Po'Lice to de-escalate a situation or to intervene when emotions are high is like calling a mortician to deliver a baby.

—Queer Matriarch La Mesha Irizarry

Transcribed from a phone call by Lisa Ganser while Mesha is at the
hospital on August 3, 2020

How Not to Call the Popo   Growing up in the sixties during the civil rights movement there is a typical saying that a black mother would tell her son, "Son, don't be walkin' with your hands in your pockets. The police will stop you and think you got a gun." I grew up with this fear of the police and that certainty of police terror runs through my veins today as an adult.

When I got raped by my roommate and a friend, I said to myself, "HELL NO, I'm not calling the police". I used another method of public humiliation. As we shared friends in common, I told all our friends and it was a constant reminder of his action. The humiliation was so great that he relocated. For one thing, living in the hood, to call the police, you would be considered a snitch. This was radical restorative justice without calling the police.

In the Black Panther Party, working at the Oakland community school, when a child broke rules of conduct or offended another student, the child who committed the offense would be brought before a council of his peers. That council of students would then be the judges regarding the issue. The offensive issue would be discussed and an agreement of action would be finalized among the council of students.

Today, we at POOR Magazine/Homefulness practice the same principles. I sit on the Elephant Council as an elder where we discuss and make decisions as a group. We then decide on various topics and situations. Some are easy and some are very difficult. Oftentimes these difficult situations need more time. We would continue until we reached common ground.

We must learn in our community of people and develop our council. We must learn to handle our own affairs. In doing this we empower ourselves. We solve our own problems and provide our own solutions. Ultimately, we avoid the capitalist financial gain of the courts and police. We avoid the financial rip off that ends up destroying us.

—Frances Moore

I'm part of the Homefulness Elephant Council because it reminds me of Indigenous traditional ways before there was a concept of police. It's a way to keep those closest to you and those within your village, accountable for behaviors that are not part of the community and world that we are trying to create. The Elephant Council created at

Homefulness is rooted in love and humanity and acknowledges that each person comes with their own baggage and gifts while holding that love also ensures the safety of the entire community. It's not easy to be accountable in a world of individualism but the concept of interdependence is our basic belief. It requires tough love, humility and a willingness to grow.

—Corrina Gould

These are not just Words No police calls, ever. These are not just words, not a slogan to be co-opted and diluted with all its meaning stripped. As part of the family elder council at Poor Magazine, it is the elders who are honored and entrusted to handle conflicts between those who make up our family, families and community—many of whom have lived with or are living in deep struggle—homelessness, police violence, landlord violence, historic violence. The conflicts that we have often come from deep trauma within ourselves. To call the police is to ignore our own agency, to give the power of our healing, our traditions, our medicines over to the same forces of police violence that have stripped and continue to strip those things away. In indigenous cultures the role of the elders is of the highest importance. This is not to say that elders do not encounter difficult situations. It is difficult to resolve serious conflict, but the elder and elder council bring wisdom and healing; it is not focused on following one elder's dictate in a hierarchical way but for the community to be heard and resolve issues that lead to justice, true justice. We refuse to call the police. We are dedicated to honoring our own judgement and agency in having the power to take control of our community by those who love, care for and value the people that live in it. In the words of POOR Magazine ancestor elder, Uncle Al Robles, "We need to take back our lives."Elephant Circle

—Tony Robles, Poverty Skola Sun of James
and Flo, Nephew of Uncle Al Robles

In the mid 1990's I became a member and columnist of Poor Magazine and as a Black, disabled young man back then, I already realized that

Multigenerational Elephant Circles

Black disabled people had and still have the second highest rate of people living in poverty (behind Native Americans) with disability. With that in mind, I was excited to learn about Poor Magazine's Elephant Circle, where poor people and others solve our own issues without guns and without taking away our housing and other needed services to live. I'm a Black disabled man who lives on SSI & section eight so I have to jump through the hoops of the system, so being on the Poor Magazine's elephant circle gives another way to solve our issues without the heavy and oppressive hand of the state.

—Leroy F. Moore, Jr.

In POOR Magazine, we have developed methods of embodying restorative practice. This occurs in a multiplicity of ways but two of the primary vehicles historically have been the "Elephant Meeting," and the "Elder Council". The philosophy is that violations of "People's Agreements" (self-determined, mutually agreed upon behavioral modes) and conflicts must be addressed head on and by community,

POOR Magazine/Homefulnes Elephant and Family Council Circles

as opposed to ignoring them; addressing them through individual confrontation, or participation in "The Man's law." From a functional perspective, these rely on a more ancient moral scheme than physical or legal coercion. They work because those called to an "elephant meeting" are so held and cared for, even during their struggles, that they voluntarily submit to the obligation of presenting before and adhering to the determinations of the community. And being real, this can take multiple meetings, setbacks can occur, and there is the chance that the process or community demands are rejected. This said, the success rate has been quite extraordinary both in terms of adherence to community judgement and in terms of healing for all parties.

The "Elder Council", though connected, is slightly different. While individual members of the "Elder Council" may participate in "elephant meetings," the convening of an "Elder Council" tends to address issues that are more serious or that implicate the fundamental structural integrity of POOR Magazine. Put simply, this is a group of long-term POOR family members who are responsible for maintaining a base-line of health and stability within the POOR family. When significant decisions or challenges are faced by the community, The "Elder Council" ensures that whatever occurs is in keeping with our core values and needs. Of note, both of these structures are deeply rooted in notions of community, justice, and self-determination, and thus there is far more room for actualization and self-defense for anyone perceiving themselves aggrieved by accusation than one would find in any courtroom. Also, the lack of reliance on coercive violence literally removes this element of violence from the entire process thus allowing for healthier resolutions and modes of being to fill the vacated space. Does this solve all issues of conflict and violence we face? Absolutely not. Are we in a healthier and less violent place than we would be either without these structures, or relying solely on "the Man's law"? Absolutely yes!

There are two takeaways from this. First, self-determination requires positive action, not just abstract thought. Second, Rome wasn't built in a day, and neither were all the indigenous communities it bulldozed over. The idea that you have to entirely solve the perennial problem of human conflict in order to legitimately critique or abolish wretched paramilitary systems like police or KKkourts is an absurd standard that these status-quo violent systems couldn't come anywhere near achieving themselves. However, we can take on the humble task of building a more liberated future. As Brother Dee would say, "Brick by Brick!". And so we have embarked...

—Jeremy Miller

As a migrante youth, I remember crossing the border when I was about 5 or 6 years old. Fom that sense of understanding early-on, I knew that the police were an institution and an entity that were there to harm myself, to harm my family, and to separate my community. Since the age of 6 years old, I never held the notion that the police or ICE existed to protect or serve our communities.

The same experience occurs to folks who have lived in poverty from a young age. There are youth between the ages of 6 and 10 who have had the sheriffs remove and separate their families due to the inability to pay the rent or mortgage. Those same youth living in poverty continue experiencing law enforcement as an institution that separates families, that harms families. The police bring instability.

These youth have been victims of CPS and they understand that these systems are linked. When these youth are victims, the sheriffs are there to reinforce the status-quo.

The same goes for folks who, regardless of circumstance, have experienced homelessness. We know about these folks from our poor-people led wesearch where we go out and collect more than just data: we collect stories, our people's stories. These adults know that law enforcement and the DPW are the people that come in and take your belongings. If you don't comply, they are there to arrest and incarcerate you.

For us folks who have lived in poverty, who grew up in poverty, who have seen policing, and neighborhood watch—we know that these entities that are supposed to "protect and serve" are actually there to criminalize us for being houseless and for being poor.

At POOR Magazine, we understand this because we've lived it. We understand and feel that the policing of ourselves and our ancestors began in 1492. There is a long history of criminalizing you if you are the other, if you don't sit politely in one of those boxes they reduce you to. Since 1492, policing has been the act of criminalizing Black and Brown folks and anything else that doesn't resemble whiteness.

When we see our folks drinking a beer or smoking a joint on the weekend, we understand that this is just some of the stuff that our folks do. Some of us are coming out of addiction, and we know we've been criminalized for our addictions. When you face that experience personally, you're less likely to criminalize someone else who is smoking a joint or drinking a beer on the sidewalk. As poor folks, it's important that we take care of each other and the different struggles that we are walking in but we don't criminalize each-other for self-medicating through the traumas of poverty. We can't criminalize or police our own folks. We who come out of poverty have a lot of trauma. We love each other and we hurt each other.

At POOR Magazine, for the last 15 years, we've been using the Elephant Circle, and other indigenous circles, to deal with some of these problems that come up in our community, in our village. When we're having a community meeting and there's a conflict or misunderstanding, we have a way of handling it. If there are two people engaging in conflict and being disrespectful, we know it's unhealthy for all of us as a village. As such, we have a protocol of deescalation,

POOR Magazine/Homefulnes Elephant and Family Council Circles

beginning with dialogue. This process can be facilitated by folks in a community who have been trained and appointed by the community and the elders.

We know that when conflicts happen, we must rise to the occasion. If someone's behavior is unhealthy during a meeting, for example, we stop the meeting. It's okay to not continue a meeting to solve everything. In this society we're told every meeting has to be problem solving. The truth is, sometimes you have to wait for the next day or the next week to keep going on the path of healing and problem solving. And first, you need to focus on deescalation.

That work doesn't just happen in meetings. It also happens in the village, in the community. It also happens personally. Here at homefulness, we once encountered a community member who had a mental break and tried to attack us. We quickly activated three members of the deescalation team who had been chosen by the community and the elders to hold these roles. Not everyone in our community is tasked with deescalating conflict. In fact, they can sometimes provoke and escalate situations if not properly trained.

For those in community, in collectives, every setting and scenario is different. These are some of the steps we take at homefulness and we put them into practice whenever these types of incidents arise in our circles. We constantly check-in about ways that we could have dealt with a past conflict better. We don't have a magic solution but we do believe in moving as a collective, as a community. It works for us, when it comes to conflict and deescalating violent encounters with community members.

We are grateful to folks like the Black Riders who have taken the time to teach our young folks and old folks about self-defense as we must be able to defend ourselves and not simply rely on the same institutions and systems that for the last 525 years have cased us, incarcerated us, and divided our communities.

Descalation and self-reliance are not easy concepts to implement but are doable when it comes to dealing with inner violence in our hoods; I know many or our comrades in the Bay Area are already practicing similar ways in their own hoods and none of this would be possible without the support of the community itself.

At POOR Magazine, we have always practiced the values of community interdependence. We don't rely on or engage with the same institutions that kill us, separate our families, and make our lifes more difficult than they already are.

—Muteado Silencio

DeeColonize Academy/Homefulness Youth & Elder Family Councils

Fixing Our Problems Non-Violently—Family Council at my school Family Council/Elephant meeting is when families and teachers identify problems and conflicts and find a way to fix them non-violently. We have many other meetings for other things like revolutionary construction.

I've been in many family councils and seen many and it has changed my personality, but this one is about some different individuals.

One day me and my brothers were just chilling talking, but some conflict happened between two girls. They were talking about some boys and a certain name came up. So Girl 1* started trash talking and Girl 2 didn't, then got offended and said something back. Girl 1 swung on Girl 2 and then they started fighting,

We were surprised; it broke out fast. Girl 2 grabbed the broom and tried to hit Girl 1 with it and they were both throwing hands. Me and the other kids were hiding in a big container because the fight got so big. Amir tried to break it up but he got punched in the face. As the fight escalated adults came.

We had our Family Council. First we read the rules of respect. There was a lot of yelling going on but we fixed the situation and Girl 1 and Girl 2 both took ownership.

Being at DeeColonize we have a lot of family councils. It's normal at DeeColonize. Family councils are the only way we can solve issues without calling the police. And having these meetings carves you different and makes you think about things unlike your old self. That way you say oh, maybe I should not do that.

We love each other at the end and there are no hard feelings. To be honest I like our system because we do non violence and talk it out without harming each other. At the end we pray as a happy big family. I am blessed to be in a school system like this because we are different. Normally there will be cops when a situation is escalated and one of the children will be harmed by the police or arrested. But we just talk.

*Specifics and personal information such as names are confidential in all family council circles at Poor Magazine/Homefulness

—Ziair, DeeColonize Academy

DeeColonize Youth Skolas Tibu & Amir

A Model for Everyone—Family Council at Deecolonize Academy   Hello my name is Amir Cornish, and I'm from West Oakland. Family Council is a meeting that solves problems that we have with each other. The organization doesn't involve the police because they don't solve problems.

Family council is an organization run by Aunties, Uncles, Grandpas and Grandmas. This is a community that solves problems within an organization called Homefulness. I have been in many of these family councils.

I even had a family council about me because a friend wrote something bad about me and we had to have a family council to resolve this problem with me and this friend. Some feelings were said and I was kind of relaxed because we got this problem out the way.

I felt safe in family council because we solved the problem and we were back to being friends. And sometimes in family council things don't go as well as we thought, but some parts are solved.

Family council is a model for other people too. We are trying to show examples to the world that we do not need cops to be involved in solving problems that we could solve within the community.

Tiny is the person who created family council for the organization, and family council involves youth and families. I learn so much from these family councils as a student and as a community member. Being in these meetings, I have changed. These meetings are hard to be in but it's worth it .

—Amir, DeeColonize Academy

POOR Magazine/Homefulness and DeeColonize Academy Family

Not Relying on the Po'Lice at all—Family Council and My Story The police, an institution put in place to serve and protect civilians, has proven time and time again that when they are called, they spell nothing but trouble for black, brown, and/or poor people in general. I am Tibu, a formerly homeless youth resident of Homefulness and a long time member of POOR Magazine. I have seen firsthand that we can't change that system, so immersed in the history of our nation that the idea of police brutality dates back to the founding of America, so at POOR Magazine we decided on a way to not rely on them at all. We are comprised of formerly homeless people of color, so calling the cops would mean a death sentence for us. So we came up with a way to solve internal conflicts without having to rely on intervention from our would-be killers. That way is a meeting/healing circle called the Family Council.

In Family Councils, we bring up the issue with both parties involved in the room and other members weighing in. These councils are regulated by a chair, who follows a guideline called the Rules of Respect. I have been in many of these, but one that specifically stands out to me is when a certain member of Homefulness slandered our name, and when confronted about it told a series of lies that involved us harming her and attempting to evict her. Over the course of this issue, there were many Family Councils and different attempts at solving the problem peacefully. Because of solutions and mediations within those Family Councils, she left. If we had called the police on her in the beginning because we were trying to get her to leave as she was not following the rules that come with living here and not contributing in any way to this project, the whole process would have been easier. However, we have no idea that if when we called the police on her, or took any sort of legal action, they might harm/kill her or us in the process, and the whole reason we came up with this process is so we wouldn't have to take that risk.

Family Councils are usually extremely uncomfortable, and long, but they are necessary for the kind of movement we are running. They perfectly encapsulate the hard work we put into making sure everyone is safe and listened to, especially the aggressors and conflict starters. Homefulness, POOR Magazine, and especially Deecolonize Academy (which I am a student of), cannot exist without the Family Council and Rules of Respect system, and due to both of those systems I can be confident in saying I have a strong grasp in problem-solving and conflict resolution. Movements like ours that consist of black, brown and poor people need resolution methods like these for survival. There is no other option, or last resort for us. We can't use one of these, but then when it becomes too difficult, call the police. We are the ones seen as enemies to this system, and relying on it to solve our problems takes the point away from our movement itself.

—Tibu, DeeColonize Academy

Chapter 4
Po'Lice/ICE Stories

Original art by Joey Villarreal created in the SHU "torture cell" at
Pelican Bay and from the book *Aztlan Realism* by Aztlan Press

Agotados | Exhausted

A statement on the 3rd year anniversary of the killing of Luis Góngora Pat by SFPD

José Góngora Pat & Luis Poot Pat

Hace tres años, hoy, 7 de abril, Luis Góngora Pat fue brutal e insensatamente asesinado por agentes de la policía de San Francisco, el Sargento Nate Steger y oficial Michael Mellone.

Three years ago, today, April 7 at 10 a.m., Luis Góngora Pat was brutally and senselessly killed by San Francisco police officers, Sgt. Nate Steger and Ofc. Michael Mellone.

La presente contiene una declaración de José Góngora Pat y Luis Poot Pat, respectivamente el hermano y el primo de Luis Góngora Pat, en el tercer aniversario de su asesinato por esos dos policías de San Francisco.

The following contains a statement from José Góngora Pat and Luis Poot Pat, brother and cousin, respectively, of Luis Góngora Pat on the 3rd year anniversary of his unaccounted for murder by those two San Francisco police officers.

Agotados

Exhausted

A mi, José Góngora Pat, me consumió el dolor de la perdida de mi hermano Luis.

I, José Góngora Pat, was consumed by the pain of the loss of my brother Luis.

A mi, Luis Poot Pat, me agotó el saber que hay mucha injusticia y no saber cómo enfrentar la perdida de mi primo Luis.

I, Luis Poot Pat, was exhausted knowing that there is great injustice and by not knowing how to make right the loss of my cousin Luis.

A mi, José, me agotó saber que la policía siempre salía justificada y me fregaba más era saber que las leyes le negaban el camino a la justicia a mi hermano.

I, José, was exhausted seeing that the police were always excused, and what messed me up the most was knowing that the laws denied my brother a path to justice.

A mi, Luis Poot Pat, me agotó mis energías, la desesperación y el coraje que cargaba mientras buscaba información sobre cómo dar con el camino a la justicia.

For me, Luis Poot Pat, my energies were exhausted by the despair and anger that I carried while searching for information on how to find a path to justice.

A mi, José, saber que ya había muerto Luis me cambio la vida y hoy confronto al mundo estresado sabiendo que a esos dos policías que lo mataron no les pusieron cargos; es una injusticia dolorosa.

Yo, Luís, pasé de ser una persona normal que veía a la policía como personas que estaban para ayudarnos a la policía como muy corruptos. Cambié para poder enfrentarme a esta sociedad en la que la policía nos está matando, nos están humillando, destruyendo nuestras familias.

A mi, José, la muerte de Luis me hizo activista. Un activista es como un periodista, que saber decirle a la gente como es que nos tratan aquí en este país. También me he hecho artista, pero no por el camino que hubiese querido. El artista es como el periodista que da una versión de los hechos, pero que al momento de compartir su visión cambia la visión de quienes miran su obra.

Yo Luis, no me considero activista. Me considero una persona que defiende sus derechos y trata de ayudar a los demás. Un activista es una persona con un compromiso más fuerte, que da su tiempo, su presencia, representando a la comunidad todo el tiempo. Por eso no me considero activista, aunque eso fue lo que hice para mi familia. Me gustaría poder ser un activista.

For me, José, realizing that Luis had died, changed my life, and today I confront the world stressed, knowing that those two policemen who killed him will not be charged; it is a painful injustice.

I, Luis, went from being a normal person who saw the police as people who were there to help us to seeing them as very corrupt. I changed in order to face this society in which the police are killing us, they are humiliating us, they are destroying our families.

For me, José, the death of Luis made me an activist. An activist is like a journalist, who knows how to tell people how they treat us here in this country. I have also become an artist, but not by the way I would have liked. The artist is like the journalist who gives a version of the facts, but who in sharing his vision, changes the vision of they who look at his work.

I, Luis, do not consider myself an activist. I consider myself a person who defends my rights and tries to help others. An activist is a person with a stronger commitment, who gives his time, his presence, to represent his community all the time. That's why I do not consider myself an activist, although that's what I did for my family. I wish I could be an activist.

Desgatamos todos nuestros recursos personales, nos quitamos del trabajo y perdimos salarios, nos endeudamos para imprimir camisetas y cartelones de protesta, para hacer vigilias y marchas, para protestar ante las autoridades.

We wore down all our personal resources, we took off from work and lost our salaries, we went into debt to print t-shirts and protest posters, to organize vigils and marches, to protest before the authorities.

Yo, José, andaba preocupado y perdía la paz y hasta la comunicación con mi familia en Yucatán por andar buscando ayuda aquí y allá.

I, José, was worried and lost peace and even communication with my family in Yucatan when I would be out looking for help, here and there.

A mi Luis, me desgastó mi vida familiar, porque no tuve tiempo para ellos sino para reuniones y protestas.

For me, Luis, this struggle wore out my family life, because I did not have time for them, but instead for meetings and protests.

Yo, José, no quería tirar la toalla, pero la desesperación me consumía cuando el fiscal no quiso ponerle cargos a la policía. Sólo pensaba: ¿De qué forma lograré que metan a la cárcel a esos policías?

I, José, did not want to throw in the towel, but desperation consumed me when the District Attorney choose not to charge the police officers. I only thought: How am I going to get those policemen jailed?

Para mi Luis, mi mayor momento de agotamiento, fue cuando el fiscal decidió no ponerle cargos a los policías. Juré que iba a tirar la toalla.

For me Luis, my biggest moment of exhaustion, was when the District Attorney decided not to charge the police officers. I swore I was going to throw in the towel.

Agotado, yo Luís, continué armado solo del coraje de querer encontrar un camino de justicia, por el cual pudiese demostrar nuestra versión real de los hechos. No es posible que no se dé a saber lo que pasó y cada momento real de trauma que nuestras familias pasamos.

Exhausted, I Luis, I carried on, armed only with the desire to find a path to justice, by which I could demonstrate our real version of the facts. It is not possible that what happened, and every real moment of trauma that our families have gone through, is not public knowledge.

A mi Luis, me levantaba el honor de ser indígena maya y luchar por nuestras vidas, nuestras familias, nuestra sangre, nuestros derechos.

For me, Luis, I rallied in the honor of being indigenous Mayan and fighting for our lives, our families, our blood, our rights.

Yo, José, cuando estaba en lo más bajo, porque no habría consecuencias, porque el Fiscal de Distrito Gascón no actúo, sentía la estaca que tenía clavada en el corazón y me surgió el coraje para seguir luchando para que la muerte de Luis no quedara impune. Luis era parte de mi. Me lo arrancaron de mi y no puedo soportar el daño que nos hicieron.

I, José, when I was at my lowest point, because there would be no consequences, because the District Attorney Gascón did not take action, I felt the stake stuck in my heart and gathered courage to keep fighting so that Luis's death would not go unpunished. Luis was a part of me. They took him from me and I cannot accept the damage that they did to us.

A mi, José, el día de la conferencia prensa dónde me desahogue en el micrófono gritándole a Gascón que era un cobarde, me desplomé aún más en la desesperación, pero al día siguiente me volvía el coraje.

For me, José, the day of the press conference, when I poured my heart out at the microphone, shouting at Gascón that he was a coward, I collapsed even further into despair, but the next day my courage returned.

Yo José, siempre digo que quede la justicia en manos de dios.

I, José, always say that justice is in God's hands.

Yo Luis, tomaba valor de nuestras creencias y de al Virgen de Guadalupe.

I, Luis, found courage in our beliefs and the Virgin of Guadalupe.

Para mi, José, cada que llegaba el día 7 del mes, día de la muerte para mi hermano, que debía levantarme al altar de la calle era como una tortura. Pero al llegar la gente y mis más cercanos colaboradores y nos poníamos al tanto de las palabras que traíamos en nuestros corazones era como una terapia para mi. Pero solo para luego regresar al dolor. Y cuando quería ya tirarme, el calor de la gente me volvía a levantar.

For me Jose, every time that the 7th of the month came around, the day of death of my brother, when I had to get up to go to the altar on the street, felt like torture. But when the people and my closest collaborators arrived and we became aware of the words we had in our hearts, it was like a therapy for me. But only to return to pain. And when I wanted to give up, the warmth of the people lifted me up again.

Para mi, Luis, cuando miraba a la gente de confianza que llegaba a apoyarnos me sentía fuerte porque sin su atención no éramos nadie frente a las leyes. Sin el apoyo incondicional de otros, que fueron como una segunda familia para mi, las autoridades no nos hubiesen prestado atención nunca.

Hoy sabiendo que agotamos todos los recursos legales, incluso la vía civil, yo Luis, me siento relajado, porque afortunadamente la esposa y los hijos de mi primo pudieron venir y tomar decisiones directas. Ya no tenía que ser su intermediario.

A mi, José, me cuesta aceptar que el caso acabo de esa forma pero acepto la decisión de mi familia. Yo quería que los policías enfrentaran un juicio, sin importar el resultado final.

Yo, Luis, quería ver que todos los hechos salieran a la luz pública para que quedará un registro público. No importaba tampoco el resultado.

Para nosotros lo más importante ahora es que se dé ese registro público de los hechos.

Yo José, fui hasta Sacramento al año pasado para apoyar la ley que ahora nos permite acceso a los registros de los policías que son acusados de abuso de poder. Este año, ejercí mi derecho pidiendo esos registros y hemos

For me, Luis, when I looked at the people we trusted, who came to support us, I felt strong because without their attention we were nobody before the law. Without the unconditional support of others, who were like a second family to me, the authorities would never have paid attention to us.

Today knowing that we exhausted all legal resources, including the civil case, I, Luis, feel relieved, because fortunately my cousin's wife and children were able to come and make direct decisions. I no longer had to be their intermediary.

I, José, find it hard to accept that the legal cases end in this way, but I accept the decision of my family. I wanted the cops to face a trial regardless of the final outcome.

I, Luis, wanted all the facts come to public light so that there would be a public record. The result of the case didn't matter.

For us, the most important thing now is that this public record of the facts be given.

I, José, went to Sacramento last year to support the law that now allows us access to the records of the police officers who are accused of abuse of power. This year, I exercised my right by requesting those records and we ganado la decisión de la corte para que me los den.

have won the court's decision that they be given to me.

Les prometemos como familia que cuando nos entreguen los registros de los asesinos de nuestro hermano y primo, se los haremos públicos para que compartan la verdad con nosotros para siempre.

We promise as a family that when they deliver the records of the murderers of our brother and cousin, we will make these public so you can share in the truth with us forever.

Hemos aprendido en estos tres años que las injusticias cometidas por la policía no son solo daños personales, sino daños sistémicos a la comunidad.

We have learned in these three years that injustices committed by police are not only personal harms, but systemic damages to the community.

Vamos ayudar a cambiar las leyes que nos han negado justicia.

We are going to help change the laws that denied us justice.

En esa lucha, nosotros sabemos que nuestros mejores aliados son las otras familias que han sufrido la misma pena, porque al igual que nosotros seguirán buscando justicia aún después de haber caido completamente agotadas.

In that struggle, we know that our best allies are the other families who have suffered a similar sorrow to ours, because like us, they will continue to seek justice even after falling completely exhausted.

Con muchísimo cariño y admiración a todos quienes nos han apoyado,

With a lot of affection and admiration to all those who have supported us,

José y Luis, de parte de nosotros y nuestra familia de guerreras y guerreros mayas.

José and Luis, on behalf of ourselves and our family of Mayan warriors.

7 de abril de 2019

April 7, 2019

www.justice4luis.org/2019/04/07/agotados_exhausted/

Untitled

Maria Moore

It was seven years ago that I received a phone call at work that changed my family's life. As I rushed home to my Dad, all I could think of was, "My sister is dead, my sister is dead, my sister is dead." That mantra ran through my frantic mind as I tried to navigate traffic while absorbing the reality that I would never see her alive again. I never got a chance to return her phone call two days before; I never got a chance to update her on the latest family gossip, and I never got a chance to keep her safe.

People of color are more likely to be victims of police brutality and the victim pool has expanded to include the mentally disabled. What is shocking, is the blatant under reporting of these killings and/or attacks. What we do know is that the numbers are increasing. Unfortunately, for any family who has a mentally disabled child, sibling, parent, friend or relative—**you cannot keep them safe**. Your love, patience, dedication, and unconditional, unbreakable resolve will not save them from what I consider the biggest threat to their lives: the police.

As a community, we need to **seek alternatives to calling the police when a person is experiencing a mental crisis**. Unless the situation is truly life threatening, inviting the police into a tense situation can lead to escalation and increase the risk of harm to the individual in distress. We need to increase the number of Mobile Crisis Teams in the East Bay. Instead of calling 911, the community should be able to access help via phone dispatch. A trained civilian point of contact in crisis situations will ensure police are not first responders and will allow for the civilian contact to take the lead and interact with the individual.

This past year has seen unprecedented organizing, action and attention around Black women's experiences of policing. However, more needs to be done to foster an environment where being a transgender woman is not a crime and not to be shamed. Unfortunately, killing a Black woman in crisis is becoming more and more common. For those with mental illness, the constant dehumanization is debilitating. Mental health issues are seen as crime issues with the need to restrain and punish as the first response.

The City of Berkeley had six years to get it right. After Kayla was killed, that was their chance to make real policy changes. What we have seen is one hour added to the hours of Mobile Crisis while the police continue to be first responders to individuals in crisis. The purpose and mission of the Police Review Commission is to protect their cops, and I must say they have done a stellar job. Even with the contempt I feel in my heart, my mind is still rational. I am here to prevent the next death, I am here for all the families who have mentally disabled loved ones. Kayla was fat, she was on drugs, she was poor, she was Black, she was schizophrenic and she was killed because of all those factors, because that's all your cops saw. What the police did not know, was that she was a daughter, she was a sister, she was an Auntie, and she did not deserve to die that night. She did not deserve to die on that floor, left exposed and uncovered, while referred to as an "IT". She was and still is an IT to you. Which is why nothing of value has been done, because the next IT your cops kill, will receive the same treatment.

In Kayla's case, the use of force could have been avoided had the officer followed her own policy. The role the police play in addressing non-violent 911 calls needs to be eliminated. The call was for a distrubance involving some one who needed to be 5150'd and off their medications. Did that person assault someone? No. Was that person clearly psychotic? Yes. The first thing Officer Gwendalyn Brown felt compelled to do before calling for an EMT or even speaking to Kayla or assessing her mental state was to run a warrant check. All the training in the world cannot change the mindset of someone who does not care to be a counselor but instead, an enforcer.

We need to seek alternatives to police when a person is experiencing a mental crisis. 35% of emergency calls in Berkeley are mental health calls and yet Crisis Intervention Training (CIT) has been trimmed down from a voluntary 40 hours of training to a now mandatory eight-hour training for all officers who are in direct contact with the public. The officers who responded to Kayla's call for mental health treatment did not have Mobile Crisis (trained mental health professionals) to assist with assessing Kayla. The officer ran a warrant check on Kayla before she finally spoke to her for approximately 5-7 minutes before attempting to arrest her on an invalid, unconfirmed warrant, for someone with Kayla's birth name, yet, incorrect date of birth. Kayla committed no crime. She was not a danger to herself or others; her roommate called for help, because Kayla needed her medication. Kayla waited over two months to see a psychiatrist in Berkeley, and when she arrived at the clinic, she was turned away, as the provider was not available to see her.

Seven years later, I feel hopeful. It has been a crushing, draining, uplifting and empowering exercise in patience that I pray will never end. What began seven years ago was a movement that gave a voice and humanity to a Black, transgender mentally disabled woman named Kayla Moore. We continue to fight for some much needed change in policy to mental health calls in the city where Kayla was killed.

Untitled

Cheri Honkala

Terror of the police is something we poor people have had to endure our whole lives.

Having to endure it for over 40 some years I will share my journey on how I went from homeless mother to one of Frontlines one in 13 people in the US being in most danger doing human rights work .

From the earliest days of a little girl I remember being snatched by the courts and on the most painful day ever, my mother was ruled unfit and I became a ward of the state. My mother did everything she could. She was very resourceful without resources and did everything she could to hang on to me. I remember oh so clearly she came to bring me her wedding flowers when I was in one of the many institutions I grew up in. She was unable to see me or leave the flowers. I watched her cry so hard from the second floor window. To this day she doesn't know how I watched her cry out in pain for her daughter. This is the day that I really came to learn that the courts, police, and social workers didn't really care about what was best for me.

Later I would begin a journey that would be about breaking unjust laws in order to keep families together.

In Minneapolis 2 blocks from where I lived, George Floyd was murdered by the police. I lived there and for many years witnessed and experienced police brutality and violence. Those of us from Minnesota knew that one day it would explode and it did.

On May 1st in Minneapolis in front of the American Indian Center on Franklin Ave we kicked off housing takeovers in the 1980's. I remember as a homeless mother going to jail sometimes 2-3 times a day. The police would come into some of the properties and hold guns to homeless people's heads. Sometimes people would piss themselves in total fear. Sometimes the police would sing solidarity songs and make us sit with handcuffs, bent on our knees in stairwells. I knew that at the height of the housing takeovers I would be killed if I didn't relocate. Minneapolis was my hometown and I would have to leave. Saturated by the political police and daily terror of dying I moved and got married and relocated to Philadelphia. The photographs of Joel Severson say it all. I would then go on to learn that police terror is everywhere especially for poor and unhoused people. In Philadelphia now I have sued the police department twice and was forced to settle out of court. I now have two boxes of unlawful arrests. That's how I got human rights defender status. It's when the police actually arrest you so many times for unlawful reasons that you actually have a reason to fear for your life and freedom. Everyday that goes by more and more encampments are swept up and more and more poor and unhoused people are locked up, beaten and killed. Most of the time it never makes the local news. Thank you, POOR Magazine, for shining a light on the daily terror of the poor. May we create a world where nobody has to live in fear.

View Insights

Promote

 Liked by **rocbookpro** and **42 others**
cherihonkala And you wonder why I'm not a fan of horror flicks. 😂Ok it's the 30th anniversary of t... more
bgaymoreoften Thank you for all you have done & continue to do to make things better Cheri 💜

May 22

 Liked by **rocbookpro** and **8,383 others**

markwebber That's my mom and that's the minneapolis police department.... 30 years... more

View all 182 comments

neekie__ 🤍 I think those that have followed you over the years since your early films knew.. We can see and feel it in your art.

View Insights   Promote

♡ ◯ ◁   • • • • • ·   ⊓

 Liked by **rocbookpro** and **42 others**

cherihonkala And you wonder why I'm not a fan of horror flicks.Ok it's the 30th anniversary of t... more

bgaymoreoften Thank you for all you have done & continue to do to make things better Cheri 🤍

May 22

Reprinted from "AmeriCaCa, the Sounds of Silenced Survivors"

Samuelin MarTinez

When I was 9 years old, my brother Nico took me with him over the bridge to pick fruit, where the rich people live. It was 1959 and my older brother let me join him and his friends. We went over the High Street Bridge that separated the Housing Projects from where 'the rich' lived, on the other side of the bay.

Every summer we would subsidize our food supply by picking fruit, from the back yards of those who had yards and fruit trees. My brother found a place where the fruit trees grew next to the street, not in back yards. I was afraid to pick fruit in the wide-open, with nowhere to run, nowhere to hide when the white people rushed out of their houses throwing rocks. So my brother knocked on the door and the lady said the trees belonged to the "public" on "public property" and the "public means everybody." "We are the public" my brother explained to me.

For the first time, since we were campesinos—farm workers, I was picking fruit and not afraid. I was hanging on to one branch and stepping on another half way up this tree with bright purple leaves. I was contemplating the new word, "public"; thinking for the first time of being accepted; in an all white neighborhood–like a miracle jus happened or something like that. The words weren't that clear but the feeling was–a feeling of relief. We didn't need a Look Out, we thought. What a beautiful lesson for a child to learn and in such a wonderful way; like a field trip that we never had in the Oakland Project School. I was stuffing fruit down the neck of my shirt. Fruit for my mother and two younger sisters was bulging at my waist. The sun was shining on these purple leaves and I was looking up at the sky through the branches, hoping to see those clouds I liked, those puffy ones.

I was feeling safe and happy, when suddenly America grabbed me by the foot and yanked me back to reality. The branch scraped the palm of my left hand as I tried to hang on and the fruit fell from my right as my head and chest thumped against branches and then the trunk of the tree. I tried as hard as I could to land on my other foot instead of my head when I came in first contact with America dressed in blue. And I saw the gun. Flat on my back I looked up at the snarling American face yelling at me in a foreign language, Americano, "What the FUCK is wrong with YOU BOY!" The biggest Americano hand I had ever seen ripped my shirt wide open and the fruit I picked for my Ama y hermanas fell to the ground.

We, the public, were picked from the ground and stuffed into the back seat of the American police car. I was crying and asking my brother, "Where are they taking us?" I felt kidnapped and was trying to understand what America was doing to us, when the side of my face was jolted by the backhand of America. The cop slapped me hard and yelled "Shut up you fukin wet back!"

My head bumped against my brother's chest and he held me, encouraging me to be quiet in his "it's not safe" warning that I was familiar with. "Keep your wet back trash on your side of the bridge!" he yelled as he pulled us from the car and we fell onto the street in the middle of the bridge; We scrambled over the rail on to the walk way. We ran back to the projects. I ran with the feeling that at any moment "they" were gonna grab me by the back of the neck and hurt me, again. I ran with a fear that would become too familiar. I ran from America and tried not to fall. I would never again get so comfortable and not be on the Look Out.

*   *   *

When I was 15 years old, our oldest brother had a new girlfriend whose parents were strict and he left the party in our brother's car to take her home before eleven or twelve. It was during this time that the police came, a lot of them barged into the house to "bust up" the party. They immediately turned on all the lights, turned off the music and had everyone up against the walls in the living room, dining room and kitchen. "Everyone show your IDs, NOW!" "If anyone is under age here, you are all in trouble!" I knew how to disappear like a rabbit and this is what I did. I slipped into one of the bedrooms and into the closet, under a big cardboard box full of clothes. I was gone.

But then I had to get out of the house. I was gonna go out the window, but it had bars and there were cops all around the house. Why, I never knew. I slipped back into the crowd of friends who had already showed the cops their identifications. Nobody had gotten arrested and the police were still looking for reasons. I snuck to the front door and could see out front, a crowd of neighbors had formed. My plan was to sneak out and blend in with them and I would not get any one in trouble because there was no way could I pass for twenty one. I hadn't even drank that much, so I was thinking clear.

I was at the screen door, when this loud cop started yelling at someone coming up the eight stairs to the front door, where I was at. It was my oldest brother trying to explain how he was late picking us up with our other brother's car. When the cop grabbed him and started yelling, "Nobody is coming in and nobody is coming out, anybody going in will get arrested with the rest!" My brother said, "I need to go in cuz I got my brother's car so what ever you gonna do to them." The cop started grunting like a wild animal, trying to throw my brother off the side of the porch to the ground below. My brother had a hold of the banister with his two hands and the cop was grabbing for his legs to fling him off head first. Without thinking I jumped out of the door and grabbed the cops arm, so he could not throw my brother off the porch. Then there was a second cop I did not see rush up the stairs and started beating on the back of my head, I was trying to protect with my shoulders and ducking.

Our married brother flew out of the house and jumped on the back of the cop that was hurting me. The banister broke and all five of us fell to the ground below. My brothers and I were quickly on our feet and now there were five or seven cops trying to beat the shit out of us. We were trying to stay on our feet and the crowd started to yell at the cops to "STOP!!!"

I was falling and my head hurt. I remember the sound of the people yelling out their protests, "Police Brutality!!!" This is the first time I heard these words. I was thinking about this as the yelling faded away and I was concentrating hard trying to hear the protesting. I was startled awake and realized I was alone in the back seat of a cop car. I couldn't remember how I got there and frantically looked around trying to see what happened to my brothers. Every time I turned to look out in another direction, a stabbing pain from my head and wrists jolted me to a stop. The handcuffs were so tight on my bony wrists.

We got charged with assault on a cop and resisting arrest. I remember standing before a judge and wanting to tell him all about what the cops did to US and how wrong it was for my brothers to be in jail for protecting each other cuz the cops were trying to hurt US real bad and the guards at this jail were trying to do the same thing the cops did. But, I decided not to waste the energy cuz I could tell this judge already made his mind up about us and about the cops.

I got a year in Juvenile Hall. We were at this place called Eighteenth and Popular in West Oakland, a condemned facility in a building that was waiting for the politics to catch up with the need for a habitable place for youth to be locked up. It was like being in an old abandoned basement: dingy, damp and cold. The first month I was locked up with my married brother, two years older than me and still a juvenile. The guards enjoyed themselves making us miserable; their taunting, pushing and bullying were all too familiar to me. What felt unbearable was having to live with not just one grown man enjoying this shit, but several, and twenty four hours a day. These bully men in uniform came in shifts, day, swing and graveyard; twenty four hours a day being taunted. My brother explained that they all read our police report and targeted us cuz they believed what the cops wrote about us. They were making an example out of us.

Being targets of hate was not new, what was new was the concentration of it in a locked facility; they had access to everything we needed and access to us all of the time.

Defund Police, Fund Humanity

Queennandi Xsheba, POOR Magazine

"We pay your salaries and you have your assault rifles ready to shoot us unarmed protesters!?!? Stop paying them, people!" A poverty skolar shouted from the crowd where about 100 people had gathered in front of the Tenderloin police station in SF to speak up against police terror, murder and blantant brutality that is swiftly plauging many states in the nation once again.

Worldwide unrest opposing the murders of George Floyd, Rayshard Brooks, Atatiana Jefferson and Ahmaud Arbery will not "quiet down" anytime soon, nor should it, because as long as the police perpetuate a form of domestic terrorism our voices shall be heard in unison demanding justice for our murdered loved ones.

While president trump was at a rally in Arizona making up racist names to replace the name of "co-vid" Rayshard Brooks was being laid to rest in a private celebration of life service in Atlanta and people including young students took to the streets in Berkeley and San Francisco in opposition of police terror.

Protesters that were at the Tenderloin police station had also called out the constant criminalization of the homeless in the city by police and other officials citing that power washing away poor people's tents without having adequate resources available for those in need with housing, mental health and substance abuse problems is not the solution to the houseless epidemic but to support those in crisis during the covid pandemic and not leave people in the streets basically to die.

The demand was to cease the abundance of funding to police departments and take some of the financial resources and redirect them into more programs that would serve the communities' needs such as education, healthcare, affordable housing, mental/drug treatment programs and most of all—equal opportunity.

"Every time there is a crisis or a state of emergency due to a disaster, poor people's lives are always looked over and swept under the rug" said one protester. "Our lives do not matter not only when it comes down to the police, but the system as a whole.", Some folks argue that if the police departments were to be defunded, that the crime rate will hit the roof because there would be no police officers to serve and protect the citizens. Unfortunately not every cop on the job "protects and serves" unless they are protecting more affluent neighborhoods and serving impoverished folks with the butt of their billy clubs-or worse.

The excuse of police brutality victims engaging in alleged criminal activities is played out and does not give authorities the right to hand out death sentences, with that said the criminal activity amongst police departments must be called out indefinitely because criminals in uniform do not deserve one red cent from the very people that they (police) oppress and kill on a daily basis.

The severe discord between the police and the black community has its history of not only brutality, but fear itself because who in the community would dare call a cop when the chief himself was the grand dragon of the KKK? The deep-seeded racism that "kept colored folk in their places" is also a tactic that conditioned black communities and other communities of color to become complacent with being victimized and refusing to report crimes out of fear of being killed and nowadays, deported and with that layer added we have a long way to go.

NOT Calling the Kkkops—EVER

How a grassroots, poor and indigenous peoples-led movement in stolen amerikkklan remains Po'Lice and devil-oper free

Tiny Gray-Garcia

"I'm going to hurt you," said one of our long-time POOR Magazine family members as he stood in the doorway of our humble office. It was a Wednesday. POOR Magazine, the poor and indigenous people-led, very grassroots, arts family has no programming on Wednesdays, so there were only four of us present: our brother who was under the influence of possibly many substances twisting his already trauma filled brain into places and spaces even he could not control; one of our disabled, houseless elders; my own houseless and under severe stress self; and another family member who struggled with multiple mental disabilities. A scenario ensued which had nothing to do with our 18 year-long, agreed to, co-created and held rules of respect, a long document with many iterations, which guides us through our mandate to Never call the po'Lice. He did not stop—substances like that don't disappear or subside quickly from your bloodstream or psyche. Instead they tend to get worse by the second. Violent words were exchanged, followed by a move by the three of us who were sober, to circle around him and guide him slowly back out of the front door. This was just one of countless times our mandate to Never call the Po'Lice was challenged physically, verbally and spiritually,

Not calling the po'Lice is hard, so hard that most people aren't ready to do it. Relying on the white supremacist crafted notion of "security" which was set up hundreds of years ago to protect the stolen indigenous territory and the settler colonizers that stole it, modeled after the "slavecatchers" of the first part of the genocidal project known as the United Snakes, is what comes easy. Not calling them, EVER, is the deep, hard, frightening and ultimately most revolutionary work.

From Betty Jones in Chicago to Cau Bich Tran in San Jose—it's not just the evil white supremacists or the benevolent gentrifiers that call the kkkops. It's often us calling these paid killers on each other. In the case of many of the most tragic stories of death at the hands of the police, it is us, the poorest, working-class, trauma-filled and most vulnerable among us that make a 911 call on each other because we often say to each other "what else can i do?"

So what else can we do?

Our ancient ways of protecting and loving each other, circling around each others' children and mothers, listening and being guided by our elders and ancestors and walking more slowly with intention, prayer and purpose have long been left in the road of hamster-wheel driven success, survival, displacement and the ache of what we have been told we must have and but can't seem to attain.

So the first answer is to do everything this white-supremacist society has told you not to do. This requires a deep mental and spiritual process of decolonization, prayer and intention which does not happen overnight or easily but rather through a long process of internal work and coalition building. This requires you to very likely "give up" the things that you have been taught will provide you with safety.

US Independence Kills—then unpack and discard what I call the cult of independence, "bootstraps" and individualism as well to resist the capitalist push to own things as a measure of happiness like cars, mama earth, clothes and jewelry.

Original art by Joey Villarreal created in the SHU "torture cell" at Pelican Bay and from the book *Aztlan Realism* by Aztlan Press

The third answer is to move back home. If your home is safe, if your families and your communities of origin are alive, help them and yourself resist the idea that you should be as far away as you can from the people who made you, who love you and who depend on you. The isolation caused by capitalism-inspired individualism can lead to mental health crises as well as setting up personally unsafe lives. Additionally, your families need you and your young self, strength, love, and connectedness to help them prevent mental health crises. American style independence kills. Your families are your elders. They can support you in moments with partners who go and get abusive. (*If your families are unsafe, then the intention of creating and being a part of a chosen family is extremely important for your survival and thriving)

Signs of the people's righteous anger during uprisings for Black Lives in 2020

The fourth answer is to not so much to give up personal safety, which for women, trans-women and children is not a possibility, but to understand deeply and spiritually that the "safety-bringers" aren't safe. Once this is clearly recognized it will prompt you to speak, collaborate, and coalesce with your neighbors, community, friends and/or families of origin or chosen families to begin accountability circles, i.e., spaces where we hold each other accountable for our actions. This is a much harder step and requires a long journey with your families and/or communities.

This idea is nothing new. It is actually very old and it's what we did as people before we had slave-catchers to "take care" of everything that "scared us". This is how we walk and live as a poor and indigenous people-led organization at POOR Magazine/Prensa POBRE, following and learning from the Black Panthers and MOVE Africa before us who refused to engage with the state agencies in place to kill and incarcerate us.

We launched POOR Magazine's No Po'Lice/CPS calls mandate when we poverty and disability skolaz began fighting for justice with La Mesha Irizarry over 15 years ago in the case of her sun who was killed by San Francisco Po'Lice after a 911 call for help. POOR Magazine family member and race and disability scholar Leroy F. Moore, Jr., Mesha, myself and many more folks worked for years on mental health training for po'Lice, but lo and behold as we see now with the tragic case of Mario Woods, mental health training doesn't really stop the paid murderers who are trained to kill us from killing us. So many layers of settler laws and post-settler protections continue to support them in their murderous ways, not to mention the kkkourts that support them once they kill, as in the horrible cases of gentrification inspired murders of Alex Nieto and Amilcar Perez Lopez. Once you are in their jails, prisons and behind their razor wires, you face more chances at their hands of murder such as the murder of Sandra Bland and so many in SF County jail.

This is why we as a group of displaced, Po'Lice harassed, colonized, incarcerated and profiled, disabled poor peoples of many nations, colors and cultures knew we could NEVER engage with the people who see us as the people to test, arrest, incarcerate and evict. We realized that we needed to create a way to hold each other with love but also discipline. The discipline launched by my strong Afro-Boriken mama who took no mess from no one and held us together as poor people because she could smell a threat, an issue, a struggle a mile away, her coming from a long line of curanderas and ancestor talkers.

After my mama passed we launched a series of circles. Our elephant circle is where we poor mamas daddys, uncles and aunties decide core issues at POOR. It is also where we tweek and re-tweek our rules of respect, which we all created and are all accountable to as it demands respect of and from all of us, no matter what nation, generation or spiritual tradition we walk from. We also launched our Family elders council and Inter—generational councils which holds our family to these principles and our core values determined in our Manifesto for Change and Declaration of Interdependence as well as our 35 page Peoples Agreement which we crafted at Homefulness to hold us to our values and principals at this sacred landless peoples movement we have created in Deep East Huchuin Ohlone land with the permission of Ohlone Peoples. There are many nuances to these circles and age alone does not mean someone is an elder.

We are not just challenged by land-stealers and the family members we love, but by our fellow community, poverty and disability skolaz who have threatened us with all manners of abuse which would lead most people and organizations to the mans kkkourts and killers. We are constantly tweeking and re-tweeking what it means to be people in trauma facing our own trauma and other people in trauma, who don't solve things by dialing those three frightening numbers or ever stepping into those kkkourts to "resolve" our conflicts.

There are other organizations like Critical Resistance who are working on this same issue with powerful anti-state movement building and a group of folks in Oakland working on a first responders "app" which is a powerful idea.

POOR Magazine poverty skolaz created the PeopleSkool program to help folks begin the long process of decolonizing their minds from the settler colonizer lies of separation, independence and "safety". PeopleSkool sessions happen twice a year in BlackAugust and January. In addition, we are planning a No Po'Lice calls workshop series—the first one will be held in Huchuin (Oakland) at the 1st Congregational Church on Sunday July 15th 3-6pm. If you would like to register for this one—please email **poormag@gmail.com**. If you are unable to attend in person we will be holding more workshops across Mama Earth to coincide with the release of POOR Magazine's Peoples TextBook: *Poverty Scholarship—Poor Peoples Theory, Art, Words and Tears Across Mama Earth*. Let us know if you would like to set up a workshop and/or book reading in your city, hood or barrio.

As revolutionary mamaz and survivors of Po'Lice, case manglers, non-profiteers, prisons and government crumbs we also work as revolutionary social workers with each other to help, protect, care for/caregive, heal, support, and peer educate our fellow mamaz, babies and elders, not ever calling CPS, (Child Protective Services and Adult Protective Services) no matter how much the system would encourage us to. This is also VERY complicated and takes both poverty skolaship and strength to realize but we believe this is necessary to truly realize the often spoken but rarely understood concept of the "village".

We are still working on a way to support our fellow sisters and brothers from domestic violence trauma and crisis and this is in progress.

Not Kkkop calling isn't easy, it seems so much "easier" to dial 911, but then again, it's not "easy" to "die" either.

Three Generations of Black Men Against Police Brutality

Leroy F. Moore, Jr.

Hello people, this is Leroy Moore. Usually I don't do, you know, solo video recordings of myself but you know, I just need to get things off my chest as we see another police brutality killing of a black man. Anyway this video is entitled "Three Generations of Black Men Against Police Brutality". I wanted to talk about that because I see the cycle that happens in the degree black men are targeted. My granddad in the 60's, my dad in the 70's and myself in the late 80's, 90's and today. All three of us fought against police brutality. And all three of us had different answers. My grandad used to say as the F the police—get them out of our community. My dad has almost the same answer.

Today, I see the community wants to do everything except getting police out of the community. Through, my like, 15-20 years of activism against police brutality (since I think 1988-1987). I've seen state answers over and over and over again. I see the answer of training. Police need more training. That started in 1989 in Memphis, Tennessee. I see that the police needs more weapons, more this, more that, more this, more that, more this, more that. It's 2020 and you know, I don't have all the answers, you know, I was there in the 80's when Elenor Bumper, an elderly disabled woman got shot in her own home. I protested and wrote letters in 1984-85, something like that.

I moved to San Francisco in '91. Idriss Stelly and Mesha, Mesha's son, Idriss Stelly. Hey guys, shout out ? told me ? on theater in San Francisco. At first, we thought that training was the answer. And only a year and we realized that we've been duped one more time and we saw that training was another statewide cycle that goes around and around and around constantly. Poor Magazine told me all these three generations, my Grandad, my father and me. And I just had to say today that you know, I'm tired of the same answers, the same cycle. Yes, protest. Yes, burn down cities. But, be honest with yourself. After three generations I know that police don't follow policies because they are protected from local judges, local lawyers, local politician, all the way up to the federal level. So if we know that the police are protected in that way, why do we always try to change the police? Poor Magazine

has a workshop called 'Never Ever Call the Police'. And we say, I say, that it's about time that the community get the money, the funds, and the resources, so that we don't have to call the police. Finally, organizations are talking about defunding the police. I've been saying that since the nineties. I go back to these three black men; my father, my granddad and myself fighting police brutality. And I wonder, am I going to pass on to my nephew? If my nephew will make a video like this and say my uncle used to fight the same fight. This is not a job. It's not a Ford Foundation Grant. It's not a movement. It's not... none of that. It goes deeper than that. It's the system that we live in because many of us have jobs in the system.

Beyond me and a police officer. Have jobs, prison guards and in all kinds of institutions that do us wrong. But because we live under capitalism, we choose to work in these jobs. I posted on Facebook, you know. Is justice just out of reach because of capitalism? And because of a j-o-b. Police brutality is more than policing. It's the whole state. And when the state pays you to go against the system that's just another job. I see movements come and go. October 22nd, Mothers Against Police Brutality and Black Lives Matter. Come and go. And we're still living under this police state. You know why? Because a lot of them don't deal with the real core of the issue because they can't because they're funded. The core of the issue is, we work in it. We're a part of it. You raise our kids to go to school, to get a job. and once you are a part of the system, It's almost impossible to eradicate. Activists get grants, book tours, film, whatever. And we see once again that this continues to happen.

About what 7 years ago, I wrote my suggestions on ending police brutality. You can go on Poor Magazine and look up Krip Hop Nation. With a K. It's like 13-14 suggestions. And not one of them deals with training. Not one of them deals with getting a job in a movement, but all of them deal with completely changing the way you live. I learned that from Poor magazine.

Like I said, they have a workshop that's called 'Never Call The Police.' It reminds me of my granddad and his philosophy back in the 70's and even 60's when my dad told me about him, saying that we don't need police. We don't need to oversee them. We don't need a committee on them. All we need is more community control and community answers. That is what Poor Magazine is doing now with no funding. You know they're building houses, growing food, have their own school, their own radio station with no funding. Poor Magazine teaching their philosophy, their experiences. After knocking on the door of the system for years and years. They realize that the answer is within them. And they are doing it. Poverty scholarship. Idriss Stelley's mother, Mesha, has been doing it for years after her son was murdered. But it's not pretty because it doesn't fit into a grant guideline. It doesn't fit into ABC or Fox News. It doesn't fit into activists climbing that ladder to get to another level. We saw that in the Bay Area. And I have to say it, Van Jones climbed that ladder. When are we going to cut that ladder off? This is not a job. It's not a career. It's not a grant proposal.

Three generations of black men against police brutality and here I am sitting at my computer in 2020 and it's still going on. We need to change our strategy. We need to know that the state has a cycle for us. The cycle for us is: They kill us. They let us protest for a little while. They handpick a few people to be a spokesperson,they get a grant. You know, they might be on Fox news or CNN. You know, the family gets a—gets a settlement. In the settlement, in the paperwork, it says that you can't protest anymore, you gotta stay quiet. So that's why a lot of the parents disappear after a year or two or three because they had to because it's in their settlement that tells you that even the lawyers for them are complicit. It's hard to say because these lawyers are activists. I know a lot of them. I like them. But they know that with these settlements parents disappear. So what do you do if you're a family? And you're in the settlement? You know, what do you do? You say no? To the money? Or do you take the money and just go on?

But it's not up to the parents. It's up to us to know the system to know that these settlements had these contracts. So we should make other underground ways of how parents can get involved without breaking that contract. But that means activists need to do things outside the system. To do things that will go against the funding. To do things that go against the so-called president. We got to do things for our children, for our nieces and nephews.

And if that means not having a job. if that means saying no to grants, if that means saying no to a media interview. then let's do it. Cause if we don't do it another person going to sit here in front of the computer and say yeah, I remember Leroy Moore. And now I'm 40-50 years old. And there's another case of police brutality. Think about it. You can go to **poormagazine.org**. Go to Homefulness, go to Krip hop Nation. You know Krip Hop did a Hip-Hop CD in a movie, a documentary called 'Where Is Hope' in 2012. We got no help for that. 'Where Is Hope' is a film about police brutality against people with disabilities. Me and Emmitt Thrower, Keith Jones. We did that. You know Poor Magazine. Lisa, I can tell you about this. Did that film, CD with DJ quad. And we didn't get any support, in the height of Black Lives Matter. What does that say? What does that say when people with disabilities have seventy percent of police shootings, but there's no Disabled activists that has a high profile—that really saying something. That say something for the whole movement around police brutality.

Because if you have 70% of your community getting shot by the police and there's not one person with a disability that has a high profile. Think about it. My friend Patty Berne started Disability Justice. If you want to know about Disability Justice go to **sinsinvalid.org**. They have the ten principles on how to practice Disability Justice. We tried talking to police brutality activists around Disability Justice, they didn't get a callback. Well, you know I'm saying today, you know, three generations of black men against police brutality. Please don't let it be the fourth generation. Let's change the system. Like we burn down our communities. Let's bring down the system. You know I think COVID is doing it but we need to do it for ourselves, but we need to do it. We need to bring down the system. Burn charity and nonprofits to these police boards. You need to burn it all down.

Three generations of black men, my granddad, my father, and me, all fought against police brutality and here I am in May 2020 still talking about the issue. That tells you that it's protected by the system by the president all the ways down to the mayor? To the judges, to the jury. It's protected. Because you can't have three generations of black men fighting for it and very little changes. That tells you that the system wants it that way and that tells you that the system is protected. protecting police so they can continue to do this. So what can we do? We can be honest with ourselves and we can really say that it's not about the system. It's about taking a step outside and really putting your life on the line and I'm talking about physical and talking about not being able to be patted on the head. Not getting the grants you wanted. Not getting that promotion you want. Not getting that book deal that you want and also practicing what Poor Magazine preaches about knowing your neighbor. That's how you change it. Yeah, it is a slow process. It's not a big movement. It's about knowing your neighbor. And say hey neighbor can I call on you?

Three generations of Black men. Don't let it be the fourth. This is Leroy Moore from Poor Magazine, Krip-Hop Nation. I just had to get that out around police brutality because like I said, it's been three generations. My granddad, my father, and me. Something needs to change. It's called the system. Peace.

West Oakland Chronicles

Boy-on-Boy Male Incest and the Demasculinization on the Basketball Courts Currently Used as a Police Precinct in the Back of Cole School with the Next Door Neighbor.

Audrey CandyCorn

Three young males no older than 11 years old were caught by the other children and the neighborhood. They began to scream and run around in disbelief for what they had witnessed on the courts. Someone was crying…it was the child that had gotten violated. I went to ask the young man what was wrong. The children spoke up for him. The word "rape" was being used. To my left were three women. I said, "Ladies, are you all aware of this current situation? One of our children has been violated…they be at y'all houses all the time." One woman turned her head. The other said "it's not my business" and the last woman said "let their parents deal with it". I walked back to the children's circle. Apparently, the little boy's own cousin who he lived with or was visiting was dry humping him and another neighbor boy pinned him down by the head.

In an attempt to empower the victim, I asked him how he wanted to deal with the situation. He was stuck. I tried to get him to go with me to his cousin's house but he wouldn't budge so I went on by myself. I hopped the fence and knocked on the door for seven minutes. No one answered. I passed the women who had refused to help and reunited with the young victim. I told him that I had nothing. Together, we went to the other boy's house that had pinned him down by the head, the one who had helped his cousin molest him.

Some kids followed. I knocked on the door of second house. The adult raising the kids shouted to get away from her door after myself and the witnesses explained to her what had happened between the boys concerning the sexual gratification against one's will. To no avail we were shooed away. It's a good thing I recorded the whole situation as it seems to me all three of these children need help and calling the police or CPS is definitely not the answer. My children and I wrote about the incident, had a family discussion and listened to the recording in hopes of learning, keeping the facts straight and helping the family.

It takes the hood to save the hood. My plan is to get the neighborhood involved now that we all know about it as there are those willing to take a stand. We have call this out amongst us coronavirus-birthing-baby-predators; the pent-up testosterone and with puberty hitting these young men that need monitoring (and so do the adults).

The silence must be broken for the medicine in the healing to flow through. Meanwhile, some of my loving brothers and sisters have agreed to help me do a workshop during the coronavirus pandemic on how not to call the police and how to keep your family healthy, happy and together, starting with this family, one at a time. It is our business. Each one reach one teach one. Join the Loveolution marathon and help. Accountability is key. Trust is a major factor and having a non-compromised safe haven is necessary. We need a department in our community that is built by the people in our neighborhood to deal with inside ghetto hood issues that get looked over due to not being able to call the police in hopes of keeping their families intact, safe and together. Often CPS is called and families are destroyed because of fear and the lack of getting the true support one needs to create a safe haven of stability without involving the courts.

We suffer in silence allowing the curse to continue. We can stop it if we choose to. Stop looking the other way. There is no better time than now especially since we're all coronavirus quarantined…

Moving in love…with a mission…

Steps we took in this incident (to avoid calling the police or CPS):

1 Bore witness
2 Recorded the incident
3 Raised awareness
4 Supported the family
5 Documented our steps
6 Need to create tool; Resource Guide of Psyche from Hood Drama as reference on how to educate.

The Re-Caging of Joey Villarreal

Poor News Network (PNN)

Joey Villarreal is an author, activist, educator, artist, community leader, and radio show host for Free Aztlan. He was distributing books in the pulga, San Jose Flea Market as he always does to make sure that the communidad, who are purposely left out, kept out, and shut down, were educated on the truth. When a friend got attacked, Joey tried to protect him and was arrested and is being held on no bail in the Santa Clara County Kkkourts under the racist, classist system of gang enhancements.

"Gang enhancements is basically a new Jim Crow law in Santa Clara County. It's pretty universal statewide, from city to city and county to county. The term that law enforcement uses is the term gang. They use the word gang, but in San Jo, we have some neighborhoods that maybe go back to the 50s, historically chicano neighborhoods, historically raza neighborhoods, or generationally called varrio, a place where the raza could basically be themselves, very culturally rich. But law enforcement will call it a gang and essentially when they call it a gang, you criminalize a whole varrio. When we allow that to happen, you know we're talking about, we're giving permission, you know, approval to criminalize our own children, uncles, grandparents, fathers, mothers, sisters. So what happens in the varrio, you know, when someone gets caught up with a crime, and when I say a crime, you know crime is only a product of poverty and inequality. Our folks, our people, you know, they may do a little dirt out of despair, out of lack of opportunity and resources, oppression right? But if you commit a crime in a varrio, you're going to get more than likely a gang enhancement, which basically means you do your time. You're responsible for what you did, if in fact you did do it, and then on top of that, sometimes the gang enhancement itself, it could turn what might be 4 or 5 year sentence into a life sentence. And sometimes the gang enhancement is longer than the actually base term itself, than the actual crime."

—Jose Valle, activist and community leader

"This is all a part of our state oppressing our people. The system has lost someone, who for 20 years of his life, was nothing but a number to them. The focus should be on these last couple of years, his actions. He became a conscious revolutionary for the community. His hard work, and selfless acts for la gente was, they were amazing, you know? You've got someone out here, who is calling you out on your stuff, speaking truth into existence, telling you in your face that the corrupt system is disproportionately and targets people of color. He speaks the truth about police brutality, what do you expect? He's now exactly where they want him."

—Christy Garcia-Irineo, community warrior

"The system, their mastermind plan with mass incarceration is to come after our people and our children. They build more prisons in our country than colleges. They're building all these prisons and who's going to fill them? Us. Joey's trying to help people move forward. Joey is fighting for our generation, and the next generation."

—Mike, Joey Villarreal's cousin

"Joey is a beloved son, father, grandfather, brother. He's being wrongfully accused of all the charges because they're trying to take away his voice. They want to silence him. My father was incarcerated all my life, our uncle. Joey's been incarcerated since the age of 12 and only got out for a few years. It's a cycle. Instead of investing in jails, why not invest in neighborhoods, in young people before they get caught up? There should be more role models out there. And that's what my brother was fighting for."

—Frank, Joey Villarreal's brother

A Whole Different Trajectory

Lisa Ganser

I used to think that when these memories play over and over, the ones that have to do with drinking/drugging or in mental health crises when kops were involved, that they are there to punish me. To show me what not to do. Today, I don't think that's true. I think I'm being shown something else...

Back in 1997, 1998, I was newly sober, for the very first time, and living in a small studio apartment in The Belmont in Minneapolis on Anishinaabe land. The Belmont (if it still exists) was a big building tucked square between downtown and uptown, on Franklin Ave, on the south side of the underpass/overpass from the Walker Art Center. It was a place I could afford. I kinda loved living there. My own place!!! I was working at the uptown Ragstock at the time. I had about a year and a half sober but I was having mental health flare ups and I relapsed.

Usually when I tell this story I talk about how I woke up in five point restraints the next morning at HCMC. I use this story to demonstrate how bad it got so fast when I drank again. BOOM, handcuffs and restraints I say. I tell the story to remind myself—don't take that first sip! I share the story with other people trying not to drink or use drugs so maybe they won't use. This morning I think there's more to it than that.

I know I was not a "good neighbor" that night. I was a human though. I went out, came back. I had my boom box cranked very loud. The landlord called a few times because of the noise and I did not turn the music down. I sang loudly to it. It was after bar close.

I had never been loud before this, at this apartment, I never had a complaint. I hate that I have to qualify myself as "good" with that statement.

I was being loud and drunk dialing people early into the morning and then I passed out and was sleeping it off.

I don't remember if the loud CD was playing on a repeat function or not while I was passed out/sleeping. That would really suck for my neighbors if the music was still blasting. Clearly something would have to be done if it was. And it's possible that it was not.

Then I was awoken by violent Po'Lice.

I have been framing this story til' now as a "consequence of my drinking." And it was, I think. And Po'Lice terror is never a "consequence of using."

Those kops ripped the door off my apartment. They woke me up and terrorized me and I freaked the fuck out and I really only remember in flashes of white light what happened. It was violent. I was harmed. The kops escalated the situation and I joined them and lost control. I was cuffed and ripped from my bed to the street. Writing this paragraph makes my heart race, so I will stop.

At some point I woke up and I didn't know where I was. I was strapped to a gurney in a hallway. Hospital staff unstrapped me. I remember feeling so sad and scared and saying "I'm sorry." I was given a bus token. I went outside. I was downtown at HCMC. I was in my pajamas and didn't even have shoes on. I hopped on a bus.

When I got home the door was completely off of my apartment. It was wide open and my cat, Tigger, was missing. My apartment was ransacked. Shortly after that I was evicted and the damage to the door was cited as one of the reasons for my eviction.

I survived Po'Lice terror that night.

Many Disabled people do not, especially Black and Indigenous folks. This is one of many stories where I survived Po'Lice terror and I know whiteness protected me. I also am impacted by the terror I survived. I accept that I was a noisy, unruly, drunk ass neighbor and that I was not responding to my landlord's phone calls. Something had to be done, in that situation.

My point today, the lesson I think I am being shown, the reframing—is that what if the Po'Lice had never been involved?

There would not have been the bruises and trauma to my body/mind, no handcuffs no restraints, the compounded PTSD from Po'Lice terror. There would not have been the property damage to the apartment door by the Po'Lice. Maybe I would not have been evicted.

If Po'Lice had not been involved

I would not have been beaten down

Suddenly UNhoused

There would have been a whole different trajectory for me.

I am being shown this life event while I have been sitting with and writing for POOR Magazine about the Po'Lice and EMT murder of white, Disabled, single Mama, Poverty Scholar and Loved One,

Vaneesa Hopson. She did not live through a similar life event here in Olympia, WA.

I'm struggling for some tripped up reason to write her story. I hear people call this "writer's block." I want to honor Vaneesa the way her sister, Crystalyn, wants Vaneesa remembered. With love. I want to weave Vaneesa's experience into the ancestor fabric of Disabled Loved Ones lost to Po'Lice murder. With rage. I've had a pen in my hand for over a year. I think maybe I'm stalled because in many ways Vaneesa's story is similar to many of mine, that I survived.

Those kops and EMTs drugged and terrorized Vaneesa in front of her apartment complex. There's video of Vaneesa's death, her neighbors were ridiculing her, she was crying out for her Mom while Po'Lice were on top of her. She was restrained and handcuffed and taken away in an ambulance. Later Vaneesa was taken off life support, surrounded by her family, the deadly dose of versed and her body—beaten by Po'Lice—the cause of her death.

REST IN POWER VANEESA HOPSON.

If Po'Lice had not been involved

Vaneesa Hopson would not have been beaten down

Buried in the ground

There would have been a whole different trajectory for Vaneesa.

Lisa Ganser is a white, Trans/NB, Queer, Disabled, Poverty Scholar tending to Squaxin, Nisqually and Chahalis land. They are a dog walker, a sidewalk chalker, and the daughter of a Momma named Sam.

Demanding Justice for Yvonne McDonald

Lisa Ganser

Black, 56 year old, former Evergreen student, activist and Loved One, Yvonne McDonald was found by a street sweeper near her home in Olympia on the morning of August 7th, 2018. Yvonne was covered in scratches, cuts and bruises; her clothes were torn, and her shoes and purse were placed eerily beside her. Yvonne died later that night at the hospital, having suffered severe trauma, hypothermia and blood loss. Yvonne's family and community are shocked and heartbroken by the sudden and frightening circumstances of their Loved One's violent death. They are equally outraged and angry at the lack of care and investigation by the shitty of Olympia. Yvonne McDonald became a "case" to Olympia Po'Lice while she was still clinging to life. The lack of care given Yvonne from first contact contributed to her death.

Instead of following leads and pursuing justice for Yvonne, the Olympia Po'Lice and koroners orifice have pushed narratives that blame Yvonne for her own death. Shitty of Olympia officials have repeatedly said that they are waiting on the tox screen results of Yvonne's body, as if having chemicals in her body justifies the violence she did not survive. Yvonne's family have been waiting for over two years with no resolution.

The city manager and Po'Lice don't return calls or information requests from Yvonne's family. The crime scene was not treated as a crime scene; there've been no interviews of potential witnesses and evidence has been lost or destroyed. Possible leads, including potential evidence of a vehicular assault, have been dismissed by the coroner's office. Yvonne McDonald survived and resisted sexism, violence, racial bias, and anti-Black racism in her 56 years. Those systematic oppressions continue after her death, with the lack of investigation by Olympia police and their co-workers at the coroner's and prosecutor's office. In life, Yvonne demanded justice for others. In death, it is others who must make this demand for her.

From Inside the Kkkage

Joey Villarreal

Starting tomorrow, Friday August 14, 2020, the Kkklanta Clara County Jail will be having a mass hunger strike until August 16, 2020. This Chicano action will include all group segments and oppressed nations people and all prisoners.

The purpose of this action is to protest the inhumane treatment of prisoners.

It's to protest the racist gang enhancements that plague brown and Black people. It's to protest solitary confinement.

It's to protest the lopsided court system, police brutality, the unjust killing of Jacob Dominguez, Antonio Guzman, Anthony Nunez, and George Floyd, and all other people unjustly killed.

It's to protest the exploitation and genocide unleashed by US imperialism around the world,

and yes, it's to protest brown children held in ICE cages by America.

We want to change the racist laws that keep brown and Black people imprisoned and labeled "gang members". The courts in the US are tools to codify national oppression and uphold colonialism. Prisoners are sending a message that we do have class consciousness and that we can organize in a positive way to effect change. Lumpen are mobilized and imprisoned Aztlan is vibrant. We are facing a pandemic. COVID means all prisoners, whether in the county jails or prisons, are on Death Row now.

The Kkklanta Clara County Jail has reached an unprecedented high in outbreak of COVID. Just in the month of August, nearly 100 prisoners have newly tested positive for COVID.

Under COVID, all prisoners are on Death Row. The death toll that we will see in prisoners will be America's Auschwitz. If we are to die of COVID, continue to be brutalized by pig violence or buried alive in the concentration camps due to the use of racist gang enhancements, we will do so fighting this injustice until the end.

The imprisoned Chicano nation realizes its vanguard role in this era, and we will continue to express our political development through the class struggle of our hunger strike. This is a protracted struggle that won't be won today, but it is a mobilization of the lumpen class. It is political education in practice.

I thank the movement, who will be here Sunday in solidarity with our action. Our efforts are for prisoners everywhere, from Aztlan to Palestine, wherever injustice is found in any concentration camp that a colonizer has built. The frontline is wherever you may find yourself, raza.

This is JV in the Kkklanta Clara County Main Jail, Black August 2020. Free Aztlan.

Original art by Joey Villarreal created in the SHU "torture cell" at Pelican Bay and from the book *Aztlan Realism* by Aztlan Press

Black Disabled Men & Police Policies 1984 to 2010

Leroy F. Moore, Jr.

Usually disability component in police brutality cases are overlooked and I was in court many times screaming inside, "talk about his, her or their disability," but it would never come up! I know I brought this up over and over again but I need to bring it up again. In the late 1990's sitting in a Poor Magazine's newsroom in San Francisco we had a well known lawyer who fights police brutality case on the people's side. This lawyer blew me away answering my question, "why when police brutality happens on poor Black disabled people there is a hash hash like no public outcry, no protest and no media?" The lawyer's reply to my question was: "Leroy, the voice of the disabled community is weak on this issue!" Now it is 2020 and I found out that disability especially Black disabled men's cases of police brutality have been weave into some major court cases that gave more power to the police and one case fought against racist polices used by police. I'm talking about Dethorne Graham, a diabetic in 1984 and Allen Moye, a blind man in 2010.

This is the facts of Dethorne Graham,

Facts of the case

On November 12, 1984, Dethorne Graham, a diabetic, had an insulin reaction while doing auto work at his home. He asked a friend, William Berry, to drive him to a convenience store in order to purchase some orange juice to counter his reaction. When they arrived at the store, Graham rapidly left the car. He entered the store and saw a line of four or five persons at the counter; not wanting to wait in line, he quickly left the store and returned to Berry's car. Officer M.S. Connor, a Charlotte police officer, observed Graham entering and exiting the store unusually quickly. He followed the car and pulled it over about a half mile away.

Graham, still suffering from an insulin reaction, exited the car and ran around it twice. Berry and Officer Connor stopped Graham, and

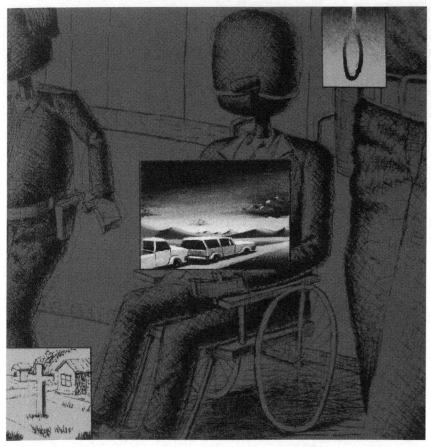

Original art by Evri Kwong, "A Nice Day for Mississippi." Edgar Ray Killian, KKK, convicted of killing three Freedom Riders in the 1960s. Courtesy of the Lannan Collection.

he sat down on the curb. He soon passed out; when he revived he was handcuffed and lying face down on the sidewalk. Several more police officers were present by this time. The officers picked up Graham, still handcuffed, and placed him over the hood of Berry's car. Graham attempted to reach for his wallet to show his diabetic identification, and an officer shoved his head down into the hood and told him to shut up. The police then struggled to place Graham in the squad car over Graham's vigorous resistance. Officer Connor soon determined, however, that Graham had not committed a crime at the convenience store, and returned him to his home. Graham sustained multiple injuries, including a broken foot, as a result of the incident.

Original art by DJ Quad

Graham filed §1983 charges against Connor, other officers, and the City of Charlotte, alleging a violation of his rights by the excessive use of force by the police officers, unlawful assault, unlawful restraint constituting false imprisonment, and that the City of Charlotte improperly trained its officers in violation of the Rehabilitation Act of 1973. The City of Charlotte filed for a directed verdict, which the district court granted. Graham appealed the ruling on the use of excessive force, contending that the district court incorrectly applied a four-part substantive due process test from Johnson v. Glick that takes into account officers' "good faith" efforts and whether they acted "maliciously or sadistically". He instead argued for a standard of "objective reasonableness" under the Fourth Amendment. The

United States Court of Appeals, Fourth Circuit, rejected this argument, reasoning that concepts such as "good faith" are relevant to determining the degree of force used. It affirmed the directed verdict, holding that a reasonable jury could not have found in Graham's favor.

Question

(1) Must Graham show that the police acted "maliciously and sadistically for the very purpose of causing harm" to establish his claim that Charlotte police used excessive force?

(2) Must Graham's claim that law enforcement officials used excessive force be examined under the Fourth Amendment's "objective reasonableness" standard?

Conclusion

No and yes. In a unanimous ruling written by Justice William Rehnquist, the Court held that claims of excessive force used by government officials are properly analyzed under the Fourth Amendment's "objective reasonableness" standard. The Court vacated the directed verdict and remanded the case to the district court to be decided by that standard.

Rehnquist noted that §1983 is not itself a source of substantive rights, but rather a means for vindicating federal rights conferred elsewhere. Rather, the Fourth Amendment stands as one of the two primary sources of protection against physically abusive government conduct, along with the Eighth Amendment. Therefore, the validity of Graham's claim must be judged by reference to the specific rights conferred by the Fourth Amendment, not by a generalized "excessive force" standard.

Justice Rehnquist rejected Connor's argument that "malicious and sadistic" is merely another way of describing conduct that is objectively unreasonable, noting that the subjective motivations of the officers are relevant under the Eighth Amendment, not the Fourth. Rather, he explained that the "objective reasonableness" of a use of force should be judged by the perspective of an officer on the scene, and should take into account factors such as the severity of the crime, the threat posed by the suspect, and any attempts by the suspect to resist or evade arrest.

Justices Harry Blackmun, William Brennan and Thurgood Marshall concurred, in an opinion written by Justice Blackmun. Justice Blackmun argued that there was not sufficient precedent to hold that claims of use of excessive force will never be subject to Fourteenth Amendment substantive due process review.
https://www.oyez.org/cases/1988/87-6571

And the facts of Allen Moye from news articles rom 2013

A legally blind black man became the first person to sue the city for unlawful use of stop-and-frisk—based on an ordeal that took place in Harlem in September 2010—following the ruling that deems the practice unconstitutional. Allen Moye of Queens says "it may be inferred" that police illegally targeted him, based on the judge's finding. The judge found the use of stop and frisk violated minorities' civil rights and ordered a monitor to oversee changes.

Moye says he was arrested on false charges while waiting for a friend in Harlem in 2010. Credit card forgery charges against him were later dismissed.

So both Black disabled men, Dethorne Graham and Allen Moye have shaped policies and fought against not only police brutality but played an important role in policies that were against their communities. Stop-and-Frisk policy was first challenged in the highest court because of a Black blind man and on the flip side the upholding of the "excessive force" standard by November 12, 1984, Dethorne Graham ruling have been giving police more gray area to continue abusing our Black, Poor and disabled communities by using "excessive force" standard as Graham experience back in his court case in the 1980's!

The Cult of the Karens vs. the Cult of the Carings

Abolishing the Karens, Carings & The Po'Lice Must include Poverty Scholarship

Tiny Gray-Garcia

> *Anti-Social Workers and Case Manglers call me Crazy, Lazy,*
> *Dumb and a Bum*
> *Cuz my knowledge don't come from the institution*
> *So How can we Abolish Po'Lice—when yo racist & classist*
> *neighbors*
> *Don't think twice*
> *Bout calling, hating, sweeping—baiting*
> *Us houseless mamas/workers/ survivors when we r sitting,*
> *standing or just waiting*
> *Abolish Po'Lice ?*
> *When Middle class people hide behind the myths of Nice?*
> *To go back to overstand & Unpack the cult of the Karens—we*
> *must overstand the cult of the Carings*
> *Anti-social workers began in business with the Po'Lice &*
> *Prisons—like they are now*
> *For Abolition to be a solution-it can't cause more poor peoples*
> *oppression*
> *For abolition to be a solution it must free up the witepeoplelies*
> *about the absence of us from your middle class eyes*
> *For abolition to be a solution we must not look to institutions that*
> *separate, preDate and destroy poor families all the time*
> *For abolition to be a solution—it must be a poor people-informed*
> *revolution*
> *Filled with sideways, indigenous life-ways—prayer , poetry and*
> *all kinds of surviving/thriving/ & liberating without more*
> *othering, silencing charity and savioring*

Today's message from a poverty skola is dedicated to poverty disability skola James Craft who wasn't killed by Po'Lice two weeks ago and all the warriors against Po'Lice terror who might not understand

and overstand that the Social Work industrial complex has acted in tandem and on their own to predate, separate, and criminalize poor and houseless families—poor black, brown and indigenous elders and black and brown, indigenous and poor wite youth. And that poor peoples theory is a necessary part of un-colonizing our minds from the lie of Po'Lice safety.

As many in the Bay Area know, an elder Black, disabled war veteran and resident of San Francisco, James Craft was surrounded by over 35 Po'Lice officers and stuck on a street corner for over 8 hours two weeks ago following a Karen/gentriFUKer (Po'Lice) call claiming Mr. Craft was holding a "weapon" and looked "menacing": classic code-words for being Black, Disabled and Poor in amerikkklan. The "weapon" was a small metal pipe—which he held whenever he was outside by accounts of other long-term neighbors who knew him. The menacing was him having a mental health crisis, and/or just being him.

"There were two DPH (Department of Public Health) workers called in and neither of them did anything, except stand by the kkkops" said Jeremy Miller, POOR Magazine Poverty skola and co-founder of CopWatch SF to Po Peoples Radio.

In the end Mr Craft was not killed mostly because of trained kkkop-watchers and poverty skolaz like Jeremy and over a hundred witnesses who were also present due to Black Lives Matter protest re-routing their march to the area. So this is a success of sorts, but how bout a complete change of that scenario, no Po'Lice, no useless DPH workers and no Karen-calls.

To begin with the end of the culture of the Karens we must go back to the origins of the Carings—aka the Caring Industrial complex known as the "settlement" houses, which were the original iterations of group homes, "closed placements" shelters and jails, these early anti-social workers were in business with the police like they are now. Getting "referrals" for "criminals" which were always poor, disabled people, oftentimes immigrants or indigenous people that they had already forced off their lands and were now setting up with free and easy alcohol access so the early day sheriffs and kkkops could arrest them.

When the Ugly laws were introduced (making it illegal to be unsightly/disabled and begging in public) the anti-social workers were the ones benefiting, the ones urging the po'Lice to pick up their future clients and bring them to the settlement houses.

These evil roots progressed into the roots of the Roosevelt launched "New Deal", created for white widows of war veterans aka the deserving poor, which the welfareQueens (WQ) uncovered in 2006, which is pretty much the same today with some racist tweeks created in the 60's. WQ—a theatre and action project of POOR Magazine— documented this through the telling of our own lives dependent on state aid, struggling, surviving through endless racist, classist norms of what and who should be a parent, how and where we should be parents and how our lives and choices were automatically viewed as suspect at best, criminal at worst.

And then there is the way the so-called "public" views poor, houseless, disabled and poor people. I intentionally left POC and indigenous out of the last list, because like my sister Jewnbug says, Poverty is a culture. Like Audre Lord says, Class Matters, and like I say, poverty is real, so yea, our loudness, our children, our life-styles, our hoopties, our stresses and our struggles are often "incomprehensible" to middle and land-stealing classes. We are often seen as annoying, a bother, messy, dirty, and/or violent when all we are is convening. As a houseless person, it's a whole nother level.

As houseless people we don't even have what I call the "privilege of privacy" and struggle with the violence of exposure, so all of our belongings and lives are on display for people to judge, hate, sweep, and profile. And in the case of disabled peoples, again our ways of being are automatically seen (or unseen) as strange, scary, or other and when you bring the ways that houselessness, disability and culture intersect with deep racist amerikkklan violence, our lives are absolutely in danger.

Witness Luis Demetrio Gongora Pat and Steven Taylor: both houseless, disabled and of color in the public, ending in their po'Lice murder.

Poverty Scholarship and PeopleSkool urgently needed in all non-Po'Lice trainings

So to take a scenario: if a person is having a mental health crisis. Due to all kinds of reasons us poor, houseless and disabled peoples have break-downs; a scam lord threat or an eviction notice, a fight with someone we love, a sweep, aka removal of our belongings while

James Craft—poverty, disability skola who wasn't killed by Po'Lice

we are living on the street, to name a few, or even more dangerous for families, a social workers referral to CPS/APS and courts systems, or even a community person who is maybe trained in de-escalation (but as my Mama Dee says, never missed a meal) might end in their death, incarceration or family separation. It is why I say the cult of the Caring—Not just the cult of the Karens.

And sometimes, there is nothing you can do. Period. Sometimes, no matter how messy, how escalated or how angry we are, we need to be left alone. Just like people inside, we need to not be "intervened" with.

In so many cases of so-called "Well-Checks" it is the reason we as poor, disabled and POC peoples end up dead. Being "escalated", Black, and a poverty skola like our beautiful Trans SisSTAR Kayla Moore, who was living in low-income housing as a formerly houseless, disabled poverty skola, was perceived as "violent" because she was having a mental health crisis, because of the structurally racist, ableist and classist gaze of the Po'Lice.

Similarly, Luis Demetrio Gongora Pat, as an indigenous houseless man was considered "violent" just because he was houseless and brown and doing what he always did in a white, middle-class, gentriFUKEd public space.

In our work manifesting the Elephant Council (the way POOR Magazine has made sure to stay Po'Lice/kkkorts and State Mandated reporter free for the last 22 years) we have had literally dozens of "encounters" with ourselves in our multi-generational villages of folks living newly inside and so many still outside, that include actual violence, escalations, extreme depression, and threats to children, elders and adults. The Elephant Council, as we teach on in the How To Not Call Po'Lice EVER workshops, has always dealt with these multitude of crisis interactions in our Poverty Scholarship–informed ways and have managed to take care of escalations, violence and trauma, which as poor and colonized peoples we sadly perpetrate often on each other and our children.

I'm so excited by MH response group that is being born out of Anti-Po'Lice Terror project and the community response teams being planned for Seattle, and all the anti-police movements coming up now in cities across this stolen land but in all of these cases I hope that Poverty Scholarship specifically is sought out, rather than just a flip to the Social Work Industry, which is NEVER poverty Scholarship Informed.

The Anti-Social Work industry (which we teach on in PeopleSkool) is rooted in white-hetero-patriarchal theory and our lives as poor, houseless and traumatized people is rarely if ever overstood by

Anti-Social Workers or even conscious, middle-class care-givers and so Po'Lice or not, our bodies, lives, children and families are always at risk of separation, mis-diagnosis and increased trauma without a deeper grasp of Poverty Scholarship, which for us poor people is "our Life".

Information on PeopleSkool's next DeGentriFUKation/ Decolonization Seminar, where we teach, speak and share Poverty Scholarship, can be found at **www.racepovertymediajustice.org.** To get an e-book or physical copy of *Poverty Scholarship: Poor People-Led Theory, Art, Words and Tears Across Mama Earth*, go to **www. poorpress.net.**

To schedule one of our workshops for your street-corner, church, comeUnity or University classroom/zoom-room, email **poormag@ gmail.com**

Open Letter to SF

Dr. Rupa Marya

August 2011

This is an open letter to SF after the police murder of one of my former patients, Charles Hill.

Charles Hill, officer that murdered Charles Hill, and peaceful protestor holding image of Charles H.

Dear San Francisco,

I am one of your local physicians and have taken care of many different kinds of people during the past nine years of my appointment as an internist at UCSF, where I have worked at SF General Hospital as well as at the VA and the UCSF campuses. San Francisco is a surprisingly small town/city?, and when you spend enough time in the healthcare industry, you come to recognize many of the city's residents. You hold their stories and watch over them in the hospital when they are ill or in the chance occurrences of running into them on the streets, in the market or painting the town red. It is an honor and great privilege to take care of the people of this city that I love so dearly.

Last month, I learned that one of my former patients, Charles Hill, was shot and killed by BART police. Per the police, he was armed with a bottle and a knife and had menacing behavior. Per eye witnesses, he was altered and appeared to be intoxicated but did not represent a lethal danger. I remember Charles vividly, having taken care of him several times in the Revolving Door, which is the health care system for the people who do not fit neatly into society. Charles was a member of the invisible class of people in SF–mentally ill, unhoused and not reliably connected to the help he needed. While I had seen him agitated before and while I can't speak to all of his behavior, I never would have described him as threatening in such a way as to warrant the use of deadly force. We often have to deal with agitated, sometimes even violent patients in the hospital. Through teamwork, tools and training, we have not had to fatally wound our patients in order to subdue them. I understand the police are there to protect us and react to the situation around them, but I wonder why the officer who shot Charles did not aim for the leg if he felt the need to use a gun, instead of his vital organs. I wonder if he possessed other training methods to subdue an agitated man with a knife or bottle.

I feel this situation quite deeply. It is hard to watch our civil servants (police) brutally handle a person and their body, when i spend my time and energy as a civil servant (physician) honoring the dignity of that person, regardless of their race or social class, their beliefs or their affiliations. I know it is not my job nor the police's job, to mete out justice or judgment of a person's worth. It is also hard because Charles has no voice, no one to speak for him now that he is gone. It would be easy to let this slide and move on with our busy lives, as we all struggle to make ends meet in this expensive city during a recession. I believe this situation shows us how powerless we all feel to some degree.

I feel outraged and am trying to find the best ways to express it–through creative outpouring and through conversations. I would like to lend my voice to the growing protest of the BART police's excessive use of violent force. I know that weekly protests are being organized on Mondays until demands are met for BART to fully investigate the shooting of Charles Hill, disarm its police force and train them properly, as well as bringing the officer who shot him to justice. The media is portraying the annoyance of the protests to commuters more than the unbelievable horror that an innocent man was shot dead by the force that is meant to protect us. I don't want to upset commuters or be a nuisance. I would like to be part of educating and not letting this slip under the proverbial rug, in honor of Charles Hill and in order to help prevent something like this from ever happening again.

I will be present at the peaceful demonstrations on Mondays in front of the BART Civic Center station, not to prevent commuters from getting home, but to educate a population that may need to pause and think about the value a human life has and the kind of San Francisco we want to live and work in.

Thank you for your time and thoughtful consideration.

Respectfully,
Rupa Marya, MD

Intitulado | Untitled

Ingrid De Leon

 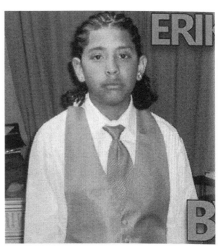

From top left: George Floyd, Breonna Taylor, Vanessa Guillen, and Erik Salgado

Hola	Hello
Agosto 3 del año 2020 mucho que contar	August 3rd of the year 2020 I have much to tell
Hace un tiempo atrás me enteré por las noticias en la Televisión	Some time ago I found out from the news on TV

Que un policía blanco mató a un hombre que se llamaba George Floyd

That a white policeman killed a man called George Floyd

Y vi cómo la gente reaccionó para que se hiciera justicia

And I saw how people reacted so that justice was done

Yo estoy de acuerdo con todas esas marchas pues da coraje ver como el policía mata a esta persona porque tiene el poder

I agree with all those marches because it is angering to see how the police kill this person because he (the police) has the power

Yo se que al igual no fueron todos los que hicieron vandalismo

I know that it was not everyone who did vandalism

Mi pregunta es unos valen más que otros ?

My question is are some worth more than others?

¿O tenemos que ver pruebas para pedir justicia?

Or do we have to see evidence to ask for justice?

Lo que quiero decir es que nadie merece morir a manos de nadie pues nadie es dueño de las vidas somo Dios es el dueño de nuestras vidas y por eso pido a las organizaciones justicia y protestas para todos o callados con todos todas las vidas valen iguales

What I want to say is that no one deserves to die at the hands of anyone because no one is the owner of lives, as God is the owner of our lives and that is why I ask the organizations for justice and protests for all or quiet with everyone all lives are worth the same

Please Don't Be Black or Brown in Alameda

Or, A Short People's History of the City of Alameda

Westyn Medicína

Dedicated to Diamond, and to all of the Black, Brown, Indigenous, Poor, Queer, Muslim and Differently-Abled residents (past, present and future) of Klanameda. You are beautiful and I love you.

I never felt like I belonged in Alameda. My features too ambiguously "ethnic". The stain of "poverty" written all over my face like the bad checks my father would have to write at the Southshore Safeway to "get us by" for a few more days. My voice, my stature…always too alluringly feminine. My ideas too radical.

It remains such an odd sensation to simultaneously call Alameda my "hometown" despite never feeling the love and support of a community.

Alameda's reputation however is that of small town quaintness, often praised for its tranquility, safety and "family-friendly" atmosphere. An island-town famous for its annual 4th of July parade and for familial strolls down "Christmas Tree Lane" in the wintertime. With its tree-lined streets and well-lit boulevards, Alameda is the perfect slice of Americana: a sanctuary for the white, wealthy, military families of the East Bay fleeing the masses of impoverished Black and Brown *peasants* just over the bridge in Oakland and beyond.

I never understood how someone could grow up in a town their entire life but never truly feel like a member of that community, until May 23rd, 2020.

On May 23rd, a cell phone recording of Mali Watkins' arrested for "dancing in the street" by no less than five Alameda police officers went viral.

And that's when I knew. That's when it all aligned for me. I realized in that instance what countless folks across the Bay Area have known (and experienced) their entire lives, that Alameda is a horrifically racist and classist town and always has been.

The Naval Station in Alameda was in operation from 1940 to 1997. Despite its closure, Alameda still maintains a mysterious "United States Naval Operations Support Center" on Clement Avenue, patrolled by heavily-armed military personnel.

With such a substantial tie to the military-industrial complex, it's no wonder that Alameda has never felt like a home for so many of us. Although there are pockets of Pacific Islanders, Afghans, Yemenis, Eritreans, Bosnians…we are the second-class citizens of Alameda, typically appropriated into the low-income housing sectors on the West End and the (now toxic) "Base" while the wealthy of the wealthy hoard their resources in Victorian mansions on Grand Street and in multi-storied homes on Bay Farm Island (yes, even the island of Alameda itself has an island).

Since Mali Watkins' arrest went viral, we've seen a calamitous response by the City of Alameda who seemed wholly unprepared to be launched center-stage into a national debate on race relations. While the police chief has since "retired" and two of the arresting officers have been placed on (PAID) administrative leave, there have been no substantial actions on behalf of official city leadership to implement the widespread change necessary to address racist policing, overt race and class discrimination and the unequal distribution of resources, that continue to scar underrepresented minorities living in the City of Alameda.

Untitled

Haleema Bharoocha

Not that this should matter, but non-Black Muslims have and consistently also experience police violence. In fact, after 9/11 state sanctioned surveillance and arbitrary detention by NYPD and other law enforcement destroyed and disrupted the lives of many Muslim Americans, Black and non-Black. As Muslim, Brown and immigrant communities, the police state has criminalized us under the guise of the "war on terror" and violent immigration policy.

We don't need policing. Many of you might argue that police are important to maintain civility and keep us safe. We must ask the question "to keep who safe, from what exactly?"

Islam has a built in model for community care. Many stories of the prophet and his companions, for example, center on ways that they took care of each other and created safety for their community. This is the model that we can build in our own communities in practicing the sunnah and teachings of Islam. For example, one teaching shared that you should know people within a 40 house radius of yours. We know that the Prophet Muhammad PBUH would not go to sleep until he knew his neighbors were cared for. "He is not a believer who eats his fill whilst his neighbor beside him goes hungry" (Bukhari). So imagine if we implemented this model now. If we knew our neighbors, we could count on them for support and safety. We should also begin to reimagine who could be called on for support in times of uncertainty.

In her latest article, Mariame Kaba discusses in depth how years of research on attempted police reforms are actually highly ineffective. Her research and work show that instead of continuing to spend billions of dollars on policing in the US, money should be reinvested into health care, housing, employment and education. In addition, she points out that there are many other ways to respond to harms in our communities, through trained mental health practitioners and social workers. Imagine if instead of calling police for every challenge, there were options to engage experts in particular de-escalation scenarios.

We argue that it is our Islamic obligation to demand and join organizing to defund the police and fund community needs. Call on me, not the cops is a great tool that you can use to share this message with your family.

The Quran commands Muslims to stand against injustice. Islamic values are deeply rooted in social justice. The Prophet (PBUH) was an anti-racist leader who stood up against a corrupt capitalist and exploitative regime to build the power of the most marginalized people in his society. We ask that you commit to anti-racism in honor of his legacy.

When The Saviors Become UnSafe

When Caring Becomes a Cage From St Petersberg to San Francisco

Tiny Gray-Garcia

Photo of the Safe Sleeping Village aka SF PeopleCage by Ken Miller

"It feels like we are back in prison, said Ronald, one of POOR Magazine's RoofLess radio houseless reporters from the Tenderloin about the cage, I mean, "Sanctuary" aka the Safe Sleeping Village that was constructed in the Civic Center of San Francisco this week for socially distant "sleeping" of houseless people while thousands of hotel and motel rooms still sit empty.

Since 1996 when myself and my houseless disabled Mama who co-founded POOR Magazine were still sleeping in bus shelters, park benches and hoopties (Mama and me were houseless for the majority of my childhood and young adulthood), we have been sharing food, money, tents and resources with fellow houseless and poor folks on the street. We are poverty skolaz, our knowledge comes from survival and we can't survive without each other. Its called Interdependence. Since Covid19 began the need has increased, more people are hungry, more people are scared and so the acts of sharing have increased with us all. The RoofLESS cru is supporting up to 700 people a week on both sides of the bay with homemade food, donated food, groceries, masks, cleaning supplies, Hand sanitizers, media and more.

POOR Magazine, the magazine and then the very grassroots, poor/ indigenous people-led movement of the same name, started cause me and Mama realized the inherent violence of this settler colonial system that criminalizes poverty and poor people like us and realized that one of the ways we had to fight back is with our collective voices, education, art and solutions. In addition to media and art, we also do something we call WeSearch—Poor people-led research—ie, not academic or CorpRape surveys, studies or tests.

"Its like Martial Law, trying to condition us, I don't feel "safe" staying there as a houseless person," said Maria, houseless reporter from the Tenderloin. Yesterday, on our Friday radical redistribution stops in SF, we launched a WeSearch project with fellow houseless folks sleeping near or in the SSV, who we have been supporting since Covid19 shelter in place pandemic began.

"I don't trust any fences, I have been in jail too long, can't go back, I just wonder where the hotel rooms they were promising are," said Marcus, RoofLess radio reporter from the Tenderloin, who was living in an alley three blocks away from the SSV. "I just hope they don't use this as another excuse to take our tents, which this city has been doing even with the pandemic.

"Have you heard of cages for immigrant children? Well they have them here for homeless people," said Pastor GW, a formerly houseless poverty skola and pastor from Mission Dei Congregation in Occupied Seminole Territory (which we call St. Petersburg).

When the Cage, (Sanctuary) showed up in San Francisco this week right after we did an action on Monday about the hoarding of hotel rooms, many of us POOR Magazine poverty skolaz, Aunti Frances Moore, Dee Allen, Leroy F. Moore, Jr., Muteado Silencio, Israel, Pearl Ubungen, Tiburcio and myself and others were brought back to our own experiences of jailing, criminalization and/or profiling for the sole acts of being a person of color, houseless and/or in poverty as well as a terrifying journey some of us went on last year to Occupied Seminole Territory aka St. Petersburg, Florida to present on the *Poverty Scholarship: Poor People-led Theory, Art words and Tears* text book, where we witnessed what Pastor Wright and Pastor GW called, The People Cages" which were actual cages of chain link fencing (just like what surrounds San Francisco's SSV) on the streets of Downtown St Petersburg.

People had to "check in" to the cages by 7pm and couldn't leave until 7am, at which point they were kicked out. Now lest you believe the Public Relations campaign by the Mayor that this is sanctuary land, let me school you. The ones who spear-headed and supported the St Petersburg one were also "helping" or Charity organizations, non-profiteers, city government and several so-called advocates, not to mention Po'Lice, sheriffs, and poltricksters.

"We used to have tent cities right down this street here in St Petersburg, me and GW were the 'street-sheriffs' making sure folks were safe at night," said Bruce Wright, formerly houseless poverty skola with the Poor Peoples Economic Human rights Campaign and pastor of the Refuge Ministries of Tampa Bay, pointing at the long empty dark street next to the "people cages."

"I can't even speak," Aunti Frances, who like me and Dee, Leroy F. Moore, Jr., and Tiburcio were all on the tour leading the workshops, have all dealt with endless criminalization of our unhoused, disabled and criminalized bodies, lives, belongings and spaces, and like Driver Plaza in Oakland where Aunti Frances deals with an endless amount of Po'Lice harassment when she operates her beautiful Black-led Self-Help Hunger Program, was still completely destroyed by this scene. "This is too much and what they want to do with all of us," she concluded.

Is this Cage or is it Sanctuary?

Many of us poverty skolaz are already clear that most of the "services" or "anti-social work" thats "provided" to poor people and why I re-name it anti-social work is rooted in violent scarcity, I.e., how little we can provide poor peoples versus how much is needed by a person or family to survive, and the criminalizing of our lives and actions and homes with constant inspections, evaluations, applications and assessments and the slippery slope of shelter beds and SRO's that require check-ins, check-outs, ID's and more. So really the 9 foot fence around a parking lot thats now called a "safe sleeping sanctuary" isn't that different from any of the soft cages built for poor people including the ultimate cage thats now the biggest "public housing project" for 89-90% of disabled, very low-income and/or peoples of color in this occupied land, aka Prisons and jails.

Nor is it any different from the hater solution to Covid19 of Las Vegas which threw its houseless people out fo the meager one shelter that town had and had them sleep in a parking lot, "socially distant" or the recent move of cleaning houseless people out of the New York subway only to have them cramped together in the lobbies of homeless shelters dangerously close together or going even further back because like I always say the Virus of poverty has been going on a lot longer than the virus called Covid19, the violent removal of houseless disabled people from the old Trans-Bay terminal in 2010 so the shiny new tech colonizers building Salesforce could be built to house more 20 something tech commuters, something POOR Magazine shed light on in our Stolen Land /Hoarded Resources Tour earlier this year.

To get clear about where this comes from and why people need to resist it we have to go back to the bloody settler colonial history of when the Savior and Charity industries became Unsafe and Caring became Cages. First we must go back to the roots aka the anti-poor people HIs-story to a terrifying thing called the Ugly Laws that Leroy F. Moore, Jr. and myself have written and reported on multiple times and a book by Sister shero Susan Schweik.

Ugly laws in the United States arose in the late nineteenth century. During this period, urban spaces underwent an influx of new residents, which placed strain on the existing communities. As a reaction to this influx of people who were impoverished, ministers, charitable organizers, city planners, and city officials across the United States worked to create ugly laws for their community. People charged under the ugly law were either charged a fine or held in jail until they could be sent to the poor house or work farm. The wording in the San Francisco ordinance indicates violators will be sent to the almshouse. This connects with the Victorian Era poor law policy.

The ugly laws did not restrict performances of people with disabilities for the purpose of entertainment or eliciting disgust, but rather restricted people with disabilities from mingling with the general public. Racism also played a role in the enforcement of ugly laws. In San Francisco, Chinese immigrants and their descendants were unlawfully quarantined to prevent spread of disease and epidemic

The first "social workers and shelters were known as almshouses and settlement houses and in a terrifying twist of the Charity Industrial complex essentially launching /creating and crafting their own clients, residents and purpose, which happens so much to poor people, the social workers were the ones who launched the Ugly laws in most cities, working in tandem with the Po'Lice, who would arrest poor disabled people from being poor and disabled in public and bring them to the shelters.

Cages, criminalization and policing as a solution isn't new, its just a continuation of a long process to make money off of poor peoples bodies and problems by the people who are supposedly here to "save" us, help us, house us. In the end, its why us poor and houseless people at POOR Magazine, the Poor Peoples Army/Poor Peoples Economic Human Rights Campaign,, Reclaim SF, 1st they Came For the Homeless and Where do We Go Berkeley and Moms4housing have been vehemently launching our own solutions to our own problems. Refusing the ongoing pimping, criminalizing and caging of our bodies and our problems and creating our own. It is also why

POOR Magazine is working so hard to launching homeless peoples solution to homelessness we call Homefulness, with guidance and permission from 1st Nations leaders of the Ohlone /Lisjan nation at the Sogerea Te Land Trust.

Evil Sheriff Joe Arpaio tried his racist hate tactics out on houseless people in Phoenix, Arizona before he began his terror on indigenous refugees from the other sides of the false borders, throwing up barricades around a two block area and telling the houseless people they couldn't leave until the morning, hoping ultimately we would kill each other. —Excerpt from *Poverty Scholarship: Poor People-led Theory, Art, Words and Tears Across Mama Earth*

"There's enough room to put us in a hotel or SRO (single room occupancy hotel) where they can keep us safe away from the virus. Why put us in a parking lot? That SRO could change someone's life," said Nick. (in a beautiful story by Matt Leahy of 48hills) one of the residents of whats been called by poltricksters Safe Sleeping Village (SSV) asks the question, why a parking lot when there are hotel rooms available,"

"They are still "sweeping" us in the Mission," said Miguel, RoofLess radio reportero yesterday.

If Mayor Breed wanted to continue the hoarding of hotels and not house houseless residents of San Francisco, she could have just stopped taking peoples tents and allow people to sleep houselessly without fear of arrest and belonging theft. Why put a 9 foot chain link fence with barriers up around a parking lot? (Sweeps and Belonging Theft is an ongoing struggle documented and fought by so many for so long including the warriors from the Stolen Belonging Project of San Francisco).

People Cages for indigenous children or houseless, disabled adults in San Francisco, Arizona or St Petersburg aren't ok, aren't ever ok and can't be normalized and like I always say, the slide into fascism isn't because the scary wite cheeto imposes martial law, or the "army" comes to town, its much more likely to happen in a slow bleed from the people who are supposedly there to support, save, or care for us…

C.A.R.E.

For the homeless
On some street

In Saint Pete
Looks like
A cage
For people
An open-air
Holding cell
South of Heaven,
East side of Hell,
A jailhouse with a dusky
Ceiling full of stars,
Black wrought
Iron bars
Surround the transients' reality.
Across the street
From a trailer,
S.W.A.T. monitors enclosed activity:
Crouching low,
Pacing around,
Nine-hour
Lock-down—
It was animals
That placed
Homeless ones in captivity
For no sins, away from palm trees & passers-by.
A step up from sidewalk
Tent-snatching.

—Excerpt of the poem "People Cages"
by Dee Allen / Po' Poets Project

Abolish the Other Po'Lice: Mandated Reporters

Tiny Gray-Garcia

POOR Magazine/Homefulness/DeeColonize Academy family at the SF Public Library for POOR Press book release event in 2018. Image by Peter Menchini.

"Noooooooo don't take my baaaabeeee…."

I dream those words in daymares and nightmares, the sound of my mama's screams haunt me to this day…

They were screamed by my mama when I was 11 and then again when I was 14. Two times CPS (affectionately renamed Child Separation Services by me and a lot of victims of this system that Dorsey Nunn said to think of like the Po'Lice) when they "found" us houseless and me not in school and automatically deemed my mama unfit to mama me. Reported by elementary school teachers, therapists and truant officers who were "mandated reporters", meaning the people who if witnessing "abuse" of a child, must "call it in."

This whole terrifying and real aspect of a houseless families life became the basis of my most recent Children's book, *When Mama and me Lived Outside.*

When Mama and Me Lived Outside, a children's book by Tiny available on **poorpress.net**. Original cover art by Ace Robles.

What is a mandated reporter and how are they related to the Po'Lice

If people don't know there is a state, county mandate, depending on where you are in the United Snakes, of anyone working with dependent children or disabled adults and elders requires the "reporting of any abuse witnessed" to a local Po'Lice department, Child or Adult Protective Services agency .

The rules dictating who is deemed "unfit" are rooted in ancient hetero-patriarchal society lies about who and what defines a parent and what or who defines "fitness" in regards to raising, loving, teaching and caring for your babies.

All that said, my mama was none of those things. She was a mixed race, poor, orphan with no job, minimal education, a disability and no husband. Her "husband" , my colonizer father, had taken her to divorce kkkort and accused her of being an unfit parent just to terrify her away from fighting for Any kind of child support.

Because he was a wealthy wite man, everything he said was believed, including using the length of my mama's mini skirts to prove that she was a "whore" as she used to recant to me.

All of these horrors happened all the time to women and still do, but when the CPS anti-social worker said the same thing, but now speaking about our homelessness and my mama's lack of "mental stability" it was locked in. Our only option was going underground. Getting lost, if you will, falling intentionally (as many of us poor people do) way deep in the cracks so as never to be "witnessed" again. This process of criminalizing and hiding is so treacherous and sad and part of the life as a houseless family.

From then on when we were sleeping outside on bus benches, park benches, in our cars, when we were lucky enough to have one, we were checking, watching, fearful that we would be seen, always hiding, cause once you are, people's inclination, usually coming from fear of the "other" the "unknown" or even just their loving hearts, savior-trained and CONfused is to "fix" it, solve it, cure it, cure "you" the houseless mama, child, elder, person having a "mental health crisis"—which frankly as a sufferer of mental illness, I'm not even sure what that is.

Suicidality, extreme depression, wanting to recluse, wanting to just sleep, even many forms of substance abuse, only become the public's problem because we don't have access to a roof. For most people that struggle with these issues who are housed, no-one gets in their business, calls Po'Lice on them and turns their struggle into a "mental health crisis" worthy of calling the Po'Lice, except of course in cases where "well-checks" lead to death-checks of many Black and Brown elders. But by and large a so-called mental health crisis, the ensuing struggle and any of the healing processes is afforded the privilege of privacy—rather than what I call the "violence of exposure." That violence of exposure is what killed Luis Demetrio Gongora Pat, Steven Tyler and so many more Black and Brown women and men across this stolen land.

For poor families, the violence of exposure leads to automatic Po'Lice /CPS calls, leading to families thrown in a worse place than they were, full of hoops they can never jump through as poor people who are struggling to stay alive, feed our children, and still acquire the crumbs it takes to do all these things, including endless appointments to assess our "sanity" with privileged "therapists" who have never missed a meal or lived our lives, assessments that determine our "fitness" as a parent based on aforementioned hetero-patriarchal , classist, concepts of parental "goodness" . And none of these are clear, or simple as they are created and rooted in the same system. Concepts like "in the best interests of the child" that is the guiding light of the "mandated reporter" are not clearcut—sometimes children and elders are in fact struggling in abuse and more than often we are struggling in a place of extreme non-support, and attack mode, that if switched up into a model of care and support, would change our situations completely.

My mama and me spent all night printing shirts and most of the next day selling shirts, because if we didn't we couldn't afford to pay for the motel room to stay in that night so we didnt have to sleep on the street. In addition to all of that we were filling out endless applications to get on low-income housing lists, section 8 lists and cash aid lists. This was our hustle and It was feedback loop from hell.

So if you witnessed us from the classist lens that informs all hetero-patriarchal notions of Mama—health, my mama was unfit to raise me. And yet really what she was, was un-supported to raise me. As a poor, disabled, mixed race single parent alone, with no family in this occupied land, she was doing her best. This society, which values "independence" and aloneness entrenches poverty with isolation.

But me and mama weren't operating like that—we were an indigenous mama and daughter in a family business trying really hard to survive. Entrenched poverty, truama and struggle like that doesn't end overnight because an anti-social worker separates a child from a birth parent and institutionalizes the child.

What happens to the mama? What happens to the child.

When Mama and Me Lived Outside, a children's book by Tiny
available on **poorpress.net**. Original art by Ace Robles.

Endless studies by academics have proven the connections
between foster care and prison industrial complex but very few people,
except some Black revolutionaries and my mama and her project
COURTWATCH has looked at the connections between CPS calls

and the Foster Kare Industrial Complex —the reality CPS gets a huge federal payout each time they seize a child from a parent and that the mandate of the anti-social worker is not coming from the people but rather the State and the Therapy Industrial Complex, rooted in the same racist, ableist, class-informed, hetero-patriarchal systems.

"That woman doesn't have the mama-gene", said my mama about some of the folks she worked along-side and supported, who no matter how much they were supported didnt really even want to parent, to be mamas or daddy or care-givers, because of all kinds of real ways they were un-linked, un-connected to their babies. Very subtle, very deep and something a poverty skola mama can assess through action and life, not a code in a wite-science book like the Bible of the Therpeutic Industrial Complex aka the "DSM" a book of codes telling therapists and doctor how to "code" our trauma..

This insanity and hypoCrazy causes poor children to be stolen from poor, Black, Brown and indigenous parents who are struggling on $341.00 dollars a month or maybe a little more and placed with foster families who will receive 1200-4,000 to raise that same child, locking in the institutionalized profit-making machine to keep being made off of that stolen child.

And to be clear the ideas I am presenting here aren't some Neo-liberal, social work perspectives, this narrative comes from Poverty Scholarship—a 22 year long poor people-indigenous people-led theory and practice—that took lives of struggle and resistance to figure out. That are rooted in culture and poverty, disability justice, multi-nationed eldership and the prayers of our ancestors. They can't be quantified in a "test" of sanity or mental fitness and should not be quickly inhaled and discounted. We do bi-yearly PeopleSkool sessions and ongoing consulting work with teachers, anti-social workers and care-givers who are mandated reporters to try to help them unlearn these very dangerous lies rooted in the krapitalism we all want to overturn.

And we don't just talk about this—we live it at Homefulness, a homeless peoples solution to homelessness where we refuse/resist Ever engaging with the Po'Lice, CPS or APS and Deecolonize Academy—a poor mama- and uncle-led school for houseless and formerly houseless, disabled and indigenous children. If we witness child abuse (which, just like violence and abuse of adults, happens in families in poverty ALL THE TIME) we don't look the other way, we don't enable it or pretend its not there, we pull the family in closer, we work with the our Family elders to bring healing practices and call an endless amount of Family Elder/Elephant councils (our accountability circles) to resolve conflicts in family and then straight up raise some reparations from our Bank of Come-Unity reparations for the family so money isn't there as another trigger to mama is losing it.

In the end, I am asking anti-Po'Lice community organizers, politricksters, conscious legislators, therapists, teachers and care-givers to look and listen, learn from Poverty Scholarship and the Elephant council models of Revolutionary Love Work as models to over-turn and end not only Po'Lice but its violent cousin, the mandated reporter model, and not replace it with what I affectionately call anti-social work or even "restorative justice". To realize ableist, racist, classist Po'Lice policies are in so many parts of our society and the least of which is how love and care is assessed for our children and elders. And that like Bell Hooks said, Class Matters, and like my sisSTAR skola Jewnbug says at POOR Magazine, poverty is a culture, in teaching, loving, raising, repairing and criminalizing our parents and children in poverty.

(UC) Po'Lice Terror in a Pandemic

UC Hastings Demands Sweeps of Houseless San Franciscans

Tiny Gray-Garcia

"They came by and took our tents, said we had to go and not come back or we would be arrested, you know a sweep" said Johnell, 48 , a black disabled, houseless elder and RoofLESS Radio reporter who lived in a tent at Larkin and Mcallisters streets since April when Covid19 struck. Johnell and his wife both got a tent from POOR Magazine's radical redistribution /RoofLEss radio cru who distributes masks, hand sanitizers, tents and hot meals to every one who needs it as well as poor people-led, street-based media, like we have been doing since 1996

The lawsuit seeks to compel the City to clear the Tenderloin's dangerously crowded sidewalks and to provide safe and sanitary shelter for the unhoused people who have been camping there in escalating numbers since the outbreak of COVID-19. The lawsuit was filed after many complaints from community groups and individuals to City officials failed to achieve visible results.

Two weeks ago a "lawsuit" was settled that was brought by UC Hastings—a law school located in the Tenderloin, which basically sued the City for not properly taking care of houseless people in covi19, which they didnt (leaving hundreds of people on the street while hotel rooms sat empty) but also sued houseless people for being houseless with the end result being the violence called sweeps of unhoused people in the Tenderloin.

The violence of this Krapitalist hate and PoLie Terror Un-Packed

First, UC Hastings is a classic example of what i affectionately refer to as akkkademia—a multi-million dollar funded institution who literally "owns" thousands of pieces of Mama Earth aka buildings in San Francisco's Tenderloin district slated for "The Dorm Industrial Complex" (a multi-billion dollar scam taught to people caught in what i term the "away-nation" the idea that somehow you can do better, be better, get smarter, by leaving your family and ancestors and community and everything that made you to travel thousands of miles away to another city , where you know no-one and then pay thousands of dollars to an insitutional school to "start your krapitalist life—(Things we houseless and formerly houseless poverty skolaz at POOR Magazine teach on in PeopleSkool—the Poverty Scholarship Book and other venues trying to decolonize and de-gentriFUK their lives).

All that said, the "Away-Nation" enables the filling up of these over-priced dorm rooms that add and/or cause massive displacement and evictions of poor and working class people from their long-time neighborhoods—all across this stolen land—from (Occupied Lenape Territory) Philadelphia to LA (Occupied Tongva) from Temple University to UC Berkeley while filling the pockets of the Insitutions and the devil-opers, real eSNakkes who "build them and charge exorbitant prices for them.

So although the Tenderloin is supposedly a "business district" there are thousands of working class residents, both housed and unhoused in the Tenderloin but they just aren't the kind of residents UC Hastings wants.

Private Property Po'Lice harass, move and evict Houseless Black, BRown and Poor people

One after the other since the lawsuit was "settled" UC Po'Lice and regular SF Po'Lice cars descended on the tenderloin, displacing, evicting, terrorizing, removing tents and houseless communities who had porta potties, hand-washing stations.

Just like all the BbqBecky'Speak that has led to countless Po'Lice terror calls and murders of Black, Brown, disabled and poor people across the US, the lawsuit is peppered with racist, classist words like "scared" and "unsafe" when talking about houseless people, a majority of whom are Black houseless people, who although they only make less than 3% of the San Francisco population, make up over %30 of the houseless population in the Tenderloin.

"If we didn't agree to leave they told us we would be arrested," Marvin R, one of POOR Magazine RoofLESS radio reporters reported.

"Before I was houseless i had an apartment in the TL, the rent got too damn high, now im homeless, and no I'm not leaving San Francisco, even though it doesnt seem like any of us are wanted here." said Roger C, another Black, disabled elder residents of the Tenderloin.

One after the other RoofLESS radio reporters told us they were told they had to go, sometimes they were offerred a hotel room if they agreed to a series of intense surveillance and hoops, or what i call case manglement and anti-social workers demanding paperwork and appointments and on and on.

—

In this time of Po'Lice terror resistance its so often that houseless people are not seen in this struggle, it is so often that the criminalization of houselessness continues with the insane violence called "sweeps" which happens all the time, and is not viewed as police terror, that poverty, wealth-hoarding and land-stealing are not not seen as crimes, and that these issues are even separate. From Occupied Huchuin where a sweep is being threatened tomorrow in the middle of a pandemic of houseless people from West Oakland to the Tenderloin—houselessness must be connected to this struggle against Po'Lice Terror.

Yes us houseless people are sometimes in struggle with drugs, mental illness and CONfusion. but so do housed people, they just have, as i call it, the privilege of privacy, instead of the violence of exposure.

NO people sleeping in tents isn't a solution but neither is hoarding and stealing mama earth and hoarding billions of dollars and arresting and sweeping people like we are trash.

And no we are not telling people to perpetrate the violent act of looking away, but we don't need the criminalization of the Savior Industrial Complex that only wants to make money off of our poverty, but really "See us" like the non-profits and UC hastings "pro-bono" lawyers who backed this lawsuit

So we are asking for Reparations for the Black residents of Occupied Yelamu, (Bank of ComeUnity Reparations) San Francisco who have been gentriFUKed out of their neighborhoods and streets by institutions like UC Hastings and give back that occupied and hoarded land.

POOR Magazine who has led the Stolen Land /Hoarded Resources Tours since 2016, our demand is for UC Hastings to give back one of those stolen buildings to houseless people so we can build our own solutions like Homefulness—which are Po'Lice Free movements to take back and unSell Mama Earth, and work to heal each other through our own self-determined, poor people-led solutions.

One of my sister-shero, poverty skola and reporter with POOR Magazine Junebug says Poverty is a culture and like i always say, Change Wont Come from a Savior, Pimp or an institution—Change will only come from a Poor People-led Solution...

Join UC Hastings Students, Reclaim SF, POOR Magazine,Coalition on Homelessness, Do No Harm, Solidarity SF, (some conscious) UC Hastings Students and others as we hold a rally outside of UC hastings—McAllister and Hyde streets at 3pm—to resist this Absolute Violence against houseless San Franciscans

Being Poor, Black and UnHoused in Amerikkklan

The Cult of Rehabilitation and the Racialization of Murder

Tiny aka Lisa Gray-Garcia, daughter of Dee, Mama of Tiburcio

A thumb is a terrible thing to waste
Black , poor and disabled thumbs legs and lives
are perceived as trash when u live outside

after all we are not human in your eyes
just an "unsightly" tribe—
lost our humanity & persona-alities on the curbs, inside of doorways
and on the road-side

Excuse me sir—do u have any spare change
On hard cement working cement aisles of objectified hate-

standing on street corners, working cardboard and cups
maybe a blink of your eye gets us a sliver of your disgust-filled love

"A cab driver closed his trunk on my thumb while i was helping him with luggage and then sped away, I guess i my thumb was less important than his fare," Papa Bear, POOR Magazine's panhandler correspondent reporting in our poor & indigenous led news-making circle we call Community Newsroom. His arm was trembling as he held up a huge grayish-white, soiled bandage dangling from his hand and continued. "This happened after I got the 132nd citation for sit-lie, sitting on the street, and the police told me if I came back one more time they would throw me in county jail for 6 months,"

Papa Bear, an unhoused, poverty skola (poverty scholarship is lived/learned/struggled for education—a concept we teach and speak on at POOR Magazine) had just turned 60 years old the day he lost his thumb and got yet another citation for the sole act of being unhoused and Black in amerikkklan. Papa Bear was a Vietnam vet with a metal plate in his head fighting for space between brutal stories of genocide endlessly looping through his mind. Even with his brain injury and constant pain Papa Bear had worked his entire life until his wife died and something died inside of him too, something my poverty skola, disabled mama used to call another little murder of the soul, the one that finally takes us down.

This was the last report from Papa Bear. It was his last newsroom on this side of the spirit journey. He died of a massive stroke on the same street corner he had panhandled (read: worked by POOR Magazine's definition) for years.

Sit-lie laws killed Papa Bear and like ugly laws before them have been killing poor peoples, disabled, peoples, disabled, indigenous elders and children since they were invented by the settler colonizer land-stealing class centuries ago.

I'm Papa Bear. That's my alias. My real name is Abdullah. What's coming down on the street—I know you've seen it in the papers—is Sit/Lie laws are starting to be enforced in the Haight area and big time in the Tenderloin.

The shelter beds were full. I slept in an alley. I was arrested. I had to accept the Judge's ruling. One year probation, and a stay away order from the alley I slept in. If I'm caught in the alley I slept in, I get a year in county jail.

Having your freedom taken away is the worst thing that can happen to you. Someone telling you what to do—I'm my own man.

I'm a double Vet. I spent 2 years in the army, 2 years in the Marine and too many years in Vietnam. I fought hard and worked hard for this country. I died for this country. In Vietnam, I woke up on a cot and they took me to surgery for 56 hours. I'm still hurting.

Sit/Lie law is not joke. They are promoting it big time. Enforcing it big time. In the Tenderloin, there are more black and whites (cop cars), more undercover, and everyone is enforcing Sit/Lie.

People are scared. They're terrified. You want to speak out, but people are scared. So many undercover, people are like, "man, we scared"—but you got to go to sleep soon, where you gonna go?

—A Papa Bear Panhandling Report—2013
POOR Magazine/Prensa POBRE

Anti-Poor People Laws = Racialization of Murder

All of these anti-poor laws not only come from a legacy of settler colonial derivative feudalism which has been criminalizing and profiting off of poor and disabled peoples since the beginning of time, but also from a bootstraps based racism and classism that pervades this stolen indigenous territory (Turtle Island).

The racialization of murder is never as clearly witnessed than the way it plays out in the criminalization, removal and generalized hate/ disgust of unhoused peoples. As poor, Black, Brown and Disabled peoples residing, convening, standing or sitting in public our fate blurs and blends into a legacy of eugenic (pure race) science which lives in most US people, even many so-called progressive people of color.

> *I lived at 34th and Adeline for years and I can attest that this park was the farthest thing from clean. Prostitution, drug dealing, drug use, fighting, humans defecating, and needles and strewn all over this park. It is a city hazard. I used to constantly get harassed while walking through it. This has nothing to do with fear of POC." excerpt of a series of comments made about a park where poor people convene, sit and stand in a West Oakland neighborhood undergoing high-speed gentrification*

In this society built on a puritan ethic of bootstraps individuation mixed with a blank screen of capitalist success-and corporate-crafted idea of cleanliness, first of all we are in danger if we are seen. Our lives, ways and broken bodies upset people. We have failed, we are not ok and therefore we are dirty, we are trash and therefore need to be trashed. Are trash. And like trash, disposed of.

To ensure that us, the living example of kkkapitlaist failure is never seen, law after law is adopted. New and different ways of arming police and poltricksters are adopted as laws to incarcerate us.

New and different for profit and non-profiteer corporations, funding sources, jobs and academic studies are launched, built and created to "fix us" "save us", rehabilitate us, incarcerate us and ultimately profit off of us.

Papa Bear was disabled, elder and Black in public. He also struggled with different forms of substance abuse like a lot of people who have houses do. and he did all this without the privilege of privation. The mere reminder of his purported "failure" and non-fixededness was a problem and needed to be solved. Even if it meant the death of Papa Bear.

The cult of rehabilitation is real.

The cult of rehabilitation is real and deeply embedded. It runs through even the most conscious peoples. Why can't he /she /they be ok? Why can't we just come up with yet another program, non-profit or law to "take care of it". These public examples of poverty is seen as a failure of our society. A reminder of our collective inhumanity. But actually, what even so-called revolutionaries and activists don't overstand is this is a clear reminder that capitalism is working just as it was meant to. People gave up their humanity just enough to have their guilt paid for and separated from their own human responsibilities to each other. The care, education and health of children, elders and all of us, is all something to be purchased, contracted or implemented. And your access to enough money determines your access to "good" or "bad" product. The type of elder ghetto tat you "send" your mama or grandparents to, "because it wasn't safe to leave them alone, and after you are too busy "making money" to care for them yourselves (senior citizen home) is based on how much money you have. The type of age-grade-separated school (another capitalist creation to "educate" your children so you or your elders you just got rid of or moved away from, don't have to) is based on how much money you have access to and of course the healthcare you receive from a science based on eugenics and the cutting up of poor, disabled and women of color that is only a few hundred years old instead of a thousands and makes mostly privileged people who make it into more institutional schools based on more race and class privilege, a whole lot of money, is also based on who much money you have access to.

What if I told you post-traumatic slave syndrome is real. That the trauma and disease of capitalism kills and destroys. That in the one wrong move you are out world of gentrifying cities like San

Francisco you can't make mistakes and then get another chance. That the witnessing and involvement in genocide aka war, poverty, displacement, incarceration, violence destroys people—forever. And that so many people will NEVER be ok. Will never be able to recover.

Maybe instead of building, funding and legislating more and more fixes this society could realize that the consequences of a dog eat dog system actually renders humble people, people walking softly on Mama earth, people like Papa Bear, in a permanent state of broken-ness.

But of course it didn't start with the poverty industry, it actually began with a society/system that embeds the myth of independence into all minds so that even indigenous peoples with values of eldership and care-giving become reliant on systems that separate to profit— care-give and criminalize.

In the Biggest kkkolony Cities..

In the biggest colony cities where the developers have the most to gain from selling Mama Earth like New York, Los Angeles, San Francisco— these kind of poor people hate-laws are raging through the streets to get rid of every last trace of working-class, poor, black or brown communities. White Supremacist laws like Stop and Frisk and Sit-Lie all come from the lie of Broken Windows and are followed and implemented by agents of the state already embed with racist ideologies of who gets to stay alive and whose bodies matters. Which led to the murders of Alex Nieto, Mario Woods and Amilcar Perez Lopez.

If these racialized, gentrifuked murders happen to housed Black and Brown people, people on the streets only need another law to make sure they are incessantly under attack, unable to rest, unable to sit, unable to stand while poor.

"We started the Tent City on the Sacramento City Hall steps because the attacks by the police and Dept of Public Works were relentless and these agencies are all under the mayor who wants a "clean city". People would come to our tent city almost dead with leg sores, edema and multiple health problems related to their exhaustion from moving, standing and being endlessly harassed for peeing, sitting or standing for over a

minute while homeless. Literally after 72 hours just resting and taking care of their basic needs, they were back to normal"

—Sacramento Tent City Organizer to POOR Magazine

So then the colony mayors working for the developers to make even more blud-stained dollars on buying and selling of Mama Earth, invest in more non-profiteer/savior systems to "help" remove, rehabilitate and fix all us broken peoples. Until we are no longer here.

Tent City WeSearch Statement Demand summary (see below for detail):

SF Mayor Ed Lie and Supervisor Scott Weiner claim they want "homeless people" to "go away" for the multi-billion dollar plantation sports event called The Superbowl. We the houseless, displaced gentrFUKed, evicted, criminalized, disabled and now living on the streets in Tents, Cardboard motels and tarps are demanding the return of thousands of dollars stolen by "sweeps" of our medicine and belongings as well as open land that we can set up our tents or build our own housing

Demands of UnHoused Resident WeSearchers:

- $109, 000 returned for loss of belongings
- The Immediate cease and desist of all sweeps, harassment and arrest of un-housed people for the act of sleeping or sitting while homeless
- Open and safe liberated land in Yelamu Ohlone territory (San Francisco) to set up tents and run a safe tent city or an abandoned building to build a poor people-led, indigenous people-led, self-determined housing, garden and healing project to build Homefulness—a poor & indigenous people-led solution to Homelessness. (modeled after Homefulness in Huchuin Ohlone land (Oakland)

The WeSearch Policy Group (WPG) is a project of POOR Magazine/Prensa POBRE—a poor and indigenous people-led, very grassroots, art-based movement. Please credit POOR Magazine/Prensa POBRE WeSearch Policy Group when re-printing . WeSearch is poor & indigenous people led research—not akkkademikly pimped research

This is why we as poor, black, brown and indigenous peoples refuse not only the cult of rehabilitation, refuse the ongoing criminalization of our lives and bodies in coalition with the #Right2Rest Campaign launched by our comrades at WRAP (Western Regional Advocacy Project) but the root idea that someone else can "solve" our housing, mental or physical problems for us. And like we said in the San Francisco Tent City Wars of 2016—*Give us Access to Liberated Ohlone Land or We Are Not Going Anywhere!*

A thumb is a terrible thing to waste
Black , poor and disabled thumbs legs and lives
are perceived as trash when u live outside

Homefulness is like Heaven

Amir, DeeColonize Academy Youth Skola

<u>Homefulness</u> is a community launched by Dee and Tiny Garcia. Homefulness is a safe place for people of color that could join us in the movement to free Mama Earth along with all of our Po Uncles, Aunties, Grandmas and Grandpas. I study at Deecolonize Academy—a school at Homefulness in East Oakland.

Homefulness is a place that helps homeless people on the streets. We give out food to see their smiles. They also have their own radio show led by youth skolaz and adult skolaz. Also we support our people in the streets.

Homefulness is not just a place, it's much more than a place—it's like heaven. We save lives during this pandemic, we always help our community and never stop, always help the poor. Homefulness is a place where you can feel safe.

Homefulness is different from the other schools. It is led by our community from the streets. They are also teaching the young ones how to take care of the elders in our community. Homefulness teaches so many things that are different from the regular schools.

Homefulness is a special space for all of us and this community fights the cruel injustice on our people. We are not a fake organization. We are the real deal, and we are always showing up and supporting anyone who needs our help.

Tamir Rice

Amir, DeeColonize Academy Youth Poverty Skola

Tamir Rice

Police terror is a nightmare for us young black males who have to live in fear and watch our back from the police because we don't want to die young. I know Tamir Rice was a good kid who did nothing to other people, but his life was taken too soon.

This could have been me because I had guns pulled on me and the police considered kids as adults, not as kids. Tamir was only a 12 year old child, and the officer who killed him is Timothy Loehmann, a 26-year old white dude.

Tamir Rice was a 12-year old African American boy who was at a Park Cudell Recreation Center. Tamir Rice was holding a replica toy gun, but the police didn't know that.

Tamir Rice died November 22, 2014. When Tamir had the gun in his hand at the park, the police just pulled up and saw Tamir with this toy gun, but the police didn't know the gun was a toy and is the reason why the police shouldn't have guns.

Tamir Rice was only a child when this incident took place and he died at 3:30pm. Back then white officers considered kids as grown men just like now in 2020. When they see our colored faces they think we look like men and this is a sad story to hear because another black boy lost his life to a cop.

Children and Weapons

Gun Violence in Amerikkka

Kimo, DeeColonize Academy Youth Poverty Skola

Royta Demarco Giles was a young 8-year-old black boy who was shot and killed at his local mall in Hoover, Alabama. He along with his sister, father, and mother were in the crossfire. His death is left with no answers, and I only beg to differ if we're asking the right question. Are we questioning ourselves enough and should we reevaluate our situation with our children and weapons?

Royta Demarco Giles's mother, who at this time wishes to be confidential about her identity, is quoted saying, "They took a good one," referring to her son who was shot and killed at 3 pm at a local mall called the RiverChase Galleria. The first shots were heard by witnesses at 3:18 pm. This is when 4 people, along with Royta, were riddled down with a hailstorm of bullets.

The family has been told that one suspect has been taken into custody, and the police department are confident there are more people responsible for the dramatic actions. This was not the only shooting at the Galleria. On November 22, 2018, Emantic Fitz "EJ" Bradford Jr. was shot unjustly as a black man by police with a legal weapon.

EJ's story is a different one but being similar in location and it's ties to gun violence. EJ in short was a black man in the Galleria on Thanksgiving. EJ had been shot by police because he was mistakenly taken as a suspect. The police who shot him said they thought EJ was an immediate threat and therefore was not convicted for shooting EJ.

I understand the right to bear arms is deeply embedded into the DNA of this country. Though it is hard to look at, this is the truth: the fact of the matter is people are dying and the more we can have these discussions of gun violence, the faster we can find a solution and find a light at the end of this tunnel.

Unpacked Skittles

Kimo, DeeColonize Academy Youth Poverty Skola

Trayvon Martin

On February 26, 2012, Trayvon Martin had just purchased a pack of skittles in his hometown of Sanford, Florida. This normal act of buying a snack at the convenience store was the last luxury of his life. As Trayvon was walking through the gated community of Twin Lakes, he was spotted by George Zimmerman, which resulted in a physical and fatal confrontation. This event very deeply affected me as a younger child in the 5th grade and still does till this day.

When Trayvon passed on the night of his murder, he was only 17 years old. Earlier that night he was strolling through the neighborhood of Twin Lakes. He had just finished leaving the local 7-11 not too far from his father's fiance's house. Trayvon had just bought a bag of skittles which he was holding in his hoodie while walking back to his home.

The majority of news outlets and case reports say that at 7:09 George Zimmmermen was running some errands and decided to drive through the Twin Lake neighborhood. According to his testimony George Zimmerman saw a dark silhouette he did not recognize in the neighborhood. Frightened, George decided to rely on his neighborhood watch training and called the police.

When he called he gave the description of a black male with a grey hoodie on. George, while on the phone call, says, "these a$$holes are always getting away." At this moment George lost sight of Trayvon.

George, still being on the call, tried to pursue the last location of Trayvon, which was in between the buildings of Twin Lake.

George Zimmerman, still on the phone, was told by police to wait at some mail boxes nearby. Instead of complying with the Police Department, he then proceeded to go towards Trayvon Martin. This was when Trayvon was shot once by George Zimmerman by the concealed weapon he carried.

When reading the story of Trayvon Martin, I think about the fact that I am 17 years old. I'm a part of a majority that is affected by this. How police department's usually target youth around this age and even younger, with cases like Tamir Rice, who 2 years later, would be shot and killed in Cleveland, Ohio for carrying a toy gun.

These systems of jail are set up from the beginning. Our schools are known to have a system targeting troubled youth. The amount of money for just 1 inmate even for a juvenile is $50,000. I know this from past experience being that I was once a troubled youth as well, but fortunately I had the grace of coming home with intentions of becoming better from the experience.

Homefulness #2

A Formerly Houseless child helps to build the future

Tiburcio Garcia, DeeColonize Academy Youth Poverty Skola

I am Tiburcio Garcia, a formerly homeless youth who goes to school at Deecolonize Academy. I am someone who is able to gaze along the spectrum of class, walking a fine line between privilege and poverty. I have privilege in so many ways: a loving, kind, mother who constantly supports and educates me, a community to lift me up immediately when I fall, friends who have my back, and a healthy relationship which on my part is due to the mannerly way I was raised. However, in the eyes of this government and many others, I am seen as someone with hardly anything, struggling to survive. That's why the project that was started by my mother, grandmother and everyone else at POOR Magazine is so important to me. That project is called Homefulness, and it's what's making sure me and my mother aren't homeless to this day.

Homefulness is a poor people's solution to homelessness, and we are starting another one. July 21, a day that is divisible by 3, was the day that we decided to start on the second version based off of the template of the original Homefulness, only two blocks down. I can still feel the grass snaking around my ankle and the weeds and vines getting stuck to my gloves. The air was saturated with pollen, and the sounds of weed whackers in the background were blending with the noise of cars passing by and multiple conversations. After a couple of minutes of hard work, pulling up grass and snipping particularly vicious fennel, I started to feel the sweat from my hair run down my back, and the hairs on my arm crisping. It was a "I need water right now even though I had a cup 5 minutes ago" day, and all of the students of the summer camp we were attending were working hard next to other residents of Homefulness and members of POOR Magazine.

This land that Homefulness resides on isn't an ordinary plot, and those weeds that we were cutting were going to disappear eventually because without our intervention that innocent half-pavement, half overgrown lot would have spelled doom for our community. We originally found out about this land while doing our Hoarded Mama

Earth and Community Reparations research, and we later found out that land would have become 20 luxury condominiums, bringing in a hoard of gentrifiers that would have completely changed the ecosystem of this environment, just like it did in the city I was born and raised in, San Francisco, and eventually had to move out of due to eviction caused by that gentrification.

I am formerly houseless, and in the eyes of the system, I am not privileged in the slightest. I don't see that. I know I am one of the most privileged people on this planet, because I actually get to shape history as it progresses. I am young, but I get to be a part of a project that will house thousands of families just like mine all over the world one day. On that day July 21, I got to lay the groundwork for Homefulness 2, the second homeless people's solution to homelessness that will very well house and give privilege to kids just like it did for me.

Tibu & POOR Magazine/Homefulness/DeeColonize
Academy Family at Homefulness #2

Po'Lice Terrorized For Being Houseless

My Mama's Story

Tibu, DeeColonize Academy Youth Poverty Skola

Sudden knocking in the middle of the night on the battered door of the taped together 1970 Ford Station Wagon. Lights shining through the window, so much harsher than usual against the darkness that blanketed the area where the car was parked. A scared daughter and her weary mother, tired after many of these nights, most of them ending with one of them in jail, after being nearly beaten.

"You know you can't be parked here this late," the officers always say, and as the daughter looks out the window she sees the relieved face of the neighbor with the phone in her hand, having called 911 on them as many have before. These kinds of situations happen all of the time in America, but one very similar was the killing of Luis Gongora Pat, a homeless man who had a 311 call as his execution.

As I grew up, my mother made sure I know all of these stories, telling them to me as another would tell bedtime stories to their child. She told me them, not as someone who heard about them from a friend of a friend, or someone who has seen that happen on the street and quickly walked away, but as someone who lived through them. My mother told me the story of Luis Gongora Pat, a homeless man in San Francisco who was in the same position she was, who was shot

194

and killed by police for the simple act of playing with a soccer ball on the street where a gentrifier lived. One 311 call was all it took, and one 311, or 911 call could have been all it took to kill my mother or grandmother. She was the daughter, and her and my grandmother were homeless. This is my legacy, and these are my stories.

I haven't come into contact with the police as much as my mother and grandmother have. This is due to substantially better housing situations, (meaning we actually had one, until we were evicted, and the cycle continued) my light-skinned privilege and my financial stability, which made it so that breaking the law is an actual choice for me. I don't have to steal cheese from Walgreens to feed my family, I don't have to park my car overnight secretly because I have a house to go back to. I am able to remain safe and lawful because of the privilege that comes with having a house and a life that isn't filled with constant terror and stress. However, I have had to move from house to house, not knowing when me and my mother will end up on the streets. I have lived in poverty, and it is only because of the landless peoples solution, Homefulness, that I currently have a stable living situation. Those moves and those sudden evictions were not just that. Those bred a fear within me about housing and financial stability that continue to plague my decision making and the way I see the world.

In our family, when the police are called, there is fear. We know exactly what the state organization that is meant to protect us will resort to if the situation gets a little hairy. Calling the police in our family means that as a child, my mother would be taken away because a neighbor called on my grandmother saying she saw a teenager living in her car with her mother. The police would be called because my mother and grandmother were sitting on the sidewalk for too long in too nice of a neighborhood. The police would be called because my mother at 14 didnt have a permit to sell painted clothing that would make sure they ate that week. "Little murders of the soul" as my grandmother would call them, were mostly caused when the police or other state agencies came knocking at your door.

It is illegal to be homeless in America, and police love to prey on those people living on the streets because their job allows them to. Being houseless means by the standards of the United States you deserve to be treated like garbage. As a class-based system, our government needs to have people of higher class looking down on the lower class, and that goes all the way down the ladder. Houseless people need to be stepped on by everyone else, and that oppression ends most of the time in the death of the houseless person, which to the general public is not seen like a big deal. Police are used to arresting and brutalizing houseless people on a daily basis, and my mother and grandmother very well might have ended up just like Luis Gongora if one wrong move was made.

Screams of Terror

Gun Violence and My Story

Tibu, DeeColonize Academy Youth Poverty Skola

Secoriea Turner

Over the course of my life, I have learned much about guns while laying in bed. I learned that there are guns that fire really quickly, but don't make a lot of noise. Those are light machine guns. I can usually only hear those when I concentrate. I also learned about the louder guns, the ones that usually follow up with screams of terror, and those are assault rifles. Finally, one of the least common that I hear are shotguns, which have a really loud boom and after four or five rounds created a silence that seems as if time itself stopped in that moment.

The sounds at night that I hear are sounds of gun violence. People being killed, families losing a loved one, and faces being put on t-shirts aren't a rarity in neighborhoods like the one I live in, and in the night I can hear all of it. These days, gun violence doesn't have rules. There is no "don't harm women or children" any more. Whoever stands in the way of the barrel is killed.

Over the July 4th weekend, as we all know, there are an abundance of fireworks being lit. This allows for far more gun violence and crimes using guns to be committed unchecked. That is how Secoriea Turner was killed in Atlanta on July 5th, only 4 days before this was written. Turner was killed while in the backseat of a car with her mother that was going towards her cousin's house. It was an act of senseless violence against a car amidst anger caused by the murder of Rayshard Brooks by police officers in front of a Wendy's in that area.

"Nobody helped me, I prayed to God and He didn't help me. My baby died in my arms."

Those were the words of Secoriea's mother Charmaine, who fortunately was not severely injured by the gunshots. I have heard many cases like these in neighborhoods like mine, and they break my heart every single time. In all of the neighborhoods I have lived in there have been countless unnecessary deaths of people in the community, whether due to gang violence, stray bullets, domestic violence but most of all police brutality, and not in the ways that many might think.

There have been many cases I've seen or heard of where the government provided ammunition and/or drugs to gangs to keep them fighting. Police officers would cause wars between gangs by telling one that another said this, and so on. This is police brutality. Many of these cases where the police interfered to harm the community have caused many of these deaths. In this case, I am not aware of the specifics as to why they opened fire on the car Secoriae was in, but I am aware that it had some connection to the murder of Rayshard Brooks, who was killed by the police less than a month earlier.

These neighborhoods that I grew up in aren't filled with so much violence and hate for no reason. When cities were first being mapped out, the rich white owners would use a process called redlining to section off specific areas of the city reserved for black and brown people. Those areas would purposefully have reduced funding for schools, city management, and if you are from there you would have a smaller chance at a job going forward. This is institutionalized racism that continues to this day, and has caused so much pain and hurt to powerful people, by encouraging and teaching them to hurt themselves and each other.

Eric Garner

Ziair, DeeColonize Academy Youth Poverty Skola

Eric Garner

On July 17th, 2014 Eric Garner died in New York City. He was selling single cigarettes from packs. Suddenly a NYPD officer put him in a chokehold while he was being arrested.

He said, "I can't breathe," relating to George Floyd which relates to me because I have asthma and sometimes I can't even get a breath. I know how it feels.

It was made illegal in New York for police to do a chokehold in 1993.

This story takes me to when my mom was picking me and my brother up from school and she was harassed by the police. This has happened before. She was assaulted by the police. Every time my innocent mom sees the cops she has anxiety. When cops are outside my mom can't even walk out or my mom would have flashbacks.

As a black child I was scared because "they don't see you as a child they see you as a man," said by mama Tiny. Corrupt cops are really an issue. Last week a guy from my neighborhood almost died, but thankfully the whole community was there and were screaming, "Don't shoot." He had his hands up and was doing everything they were telling him to. But then again the cops just wanted to shoot for fun and this isn't nothing new for the cops. This is a routine.

Eric was a peaceful man with a different hustle and way of "gettin it." He was married and his friends would call him the neighborhood peace maker. He was the father of six children, had three grandchildren, and at the time of his death had a 3-month-old child.

In conclusion the only way a black man will not get killed is by fitting in and being a gentrifier and we still get killed to this day. Peace and love to Garner's family. If you were raised in the hood and black you would feel this pain. Good bye.

In my Neighborhood Gun Violence is Normal

Ziair, DeeColonize Academy Youth Poverty Skola

Mama Audrey CandyCorn and Suns Ziair and Amir at San Quentin march demanding release of incarcerated peoples in a pandemic, sponsored by Prison Focus, KAGE Universal, and many more organizations.

I'm Ziair and in my neighborhood West Oakland, hearing gun fire is normal. My brother got shot in the same hood where I live, so I really know how it is to have a family member shot. In West Oakland little kids as young as 11 have and play with guns. Kids that I hoop with carry weapons.

Me and my family have been impacted by gun violence when I lost a loved one.

Natalia Wallace, age 7 from Chicago. Natalia was "sweet, shy, loving, and good at math," said her family. In Chicago, an innocent kind kid's life was taken, first degree murder. The getaway driver was found and denied bail. She was killed after being struck by a stray bullet at a family 4th of July party in the 100-block of North Latrobe Avenue.

Natalia was playing on a sidewalk when police said three armed men got out of a white car and fired more than 20 times in the direction of the people holding the party that police said included many children Natalia was killed while playing with her cousins in a yard in the Austin neighborhood.

Losing my brother Torian was horrible. I didn't think it was real. I thought no, not my brother.

Everybody knew him and he knew everybody but some envied. Torian was killed by a black on black crime. He died in a park. It was traumatizing for me because my brother smiled at me while he was in the emergency car at the same time slowly dying. It really hurt me. I never knew somebody that close would die. Little did I know that would be the last time I would see him.

Original art by Tristen H.

Gone

Luz

When artic and hades join a fight
Ice melts
Flames quell
A battle to the end.
Only thing left is a heart of stone.
With a lesson left behind.

~ PROSPERITY

Bullet to head. Over a shade of skin color skin. You play with life
because you have a badge. You think you're entitled but to me
you're nothing, the same way human lives mean nothing to
you. Race is a social construct to keep us in cages like animals
so the power lies in your hands but we are butterflies breaking
free majestically out the cocoon. We are not yours to keep
hostage. I stand next to my black kings and queens, for we are
one. Imagine not being able to breathe or make something of
yourself or life because a miserable racist took it.

~

Word to my Indigenous Kkkolonized "LatinX/Hispanic" Community

Celia Espinosa

This is not the Oppression Olympics
Take a look at our similar histories

The same type of violence that killed Breonna Taylor
killed Vanessa Guillén, George Floyd, and Erik Salgado
and many others who passed on to the spirit world

Children, Momma's, and Father's from Turtle Island
left traumatized, assaulted, and caged up by I.C.E.

Missing and murdered Native Womxn of the First Nation

Time has passed
But this type of violence hasn't
This violence is a virus
And the virus is racism

We are marching together
Raising our voices together
We must fight together
Black and Brown people must unite.

I wrote this piece because I've been seeing a lot of bullshit social media statements being shared between Indigenous brown folx "Latinx/ Hispanic's." A lot of them are from older generations of Tia's and Tio's but there are younger folx who are still in that kkkolonizer mind set of pitting themselves against our black relatives. These posts claim that no one cares about brown people and that nothing is being done to bring attention but that's NOT TRUE. Dekkkolonization is the process of learning and unlearning these white supremacist structures like anti-blackness and colorism that was forcefully taught and engrained to our minds for over 500 years… We have a lot of healing/inner work to do if we are really about taking these racist structures down. Remind and check your familia that share hate statements on social media. It's doing literally nothing because violence from the state will still be murdering innocent black and brown folx, covering it up, and getting away with it.

Palabra Para Mi Comunidad Indígenx Kkkolonizada "LatinX / Hispana"

Estas no son las Olimpiadas de la Opresión
Eche un vistazo a nuestras historias similares

El mismo tipo de violencia que mató a Breonna Taylor
mató a Vanessa Guillén, George Floyd y Erik Salgado
y muchos otros que pasaron al mundo espiritual

Niños, Mamás y Papás de Nuestra Isla de Tortuga
dejados traumatizados, agredidos y enjaulados por I.C.E.

Mujxres Indigenxs desaparecidas y asesinadas de la Primera Nación

El tiempo ha pasado
Pero este tipo de violencia no
Esta violencia es un virus
Y el virus es racismo

Estamos marchando juntos
Alzando nuestras voces juntos
Debemos luchar juntos
Los Negros y los Morenos tienen que unirse.

Escribí este artículo porque he visto declaraciones de mierda en las redes sociales que se comparten entre la gente Morena indígenx o "latinx / hispanos". Muchos de ellos son de generaciones anteriores, y son nuestros Tia's y Tio's, pero hay gente más joven que todavía tiene esa mentalidad kkkolonizador y estan a contra de nuestros parientes Negros. Estas publicaciones afirman que a nadie le importan las personas Morenas y que nadie está haciendo nada para llamar la atención, pero eso NO ES CIERTO. La deskkkolonización es el proceso de aprender y desaprender estas estructuras supremacistas blancas como la anti-negrura y el colorismo que fueron enseñadas y arraigadas a la fuerza en nuestras mentes durante más de 500 años ... Tenemos mucho trabajo interno y sanación que hacer si realmente queremos tomar estas estructuras racistas abajo. Recuerda y revisa a tu familia cuando comparten esas declaraciones de odio en las redes sociales o si dicen cosas de odio. Literalmente no está haciendo nada porque la violencia del estado seguirá asesinando a inocentes Negros y Morenos, encubriéndolo y saliéndose con la suya de asesinatos.

Remembrances

Kayla Moore—Killed by Berkeley Police Department in 2013

Steven Taylor—Killed by San Leandro Police in April 2020

On August 24, 2019 this brilliant, kind, and beautiful 23 year old black man named **Elijah McClain** was walking home when someone called 911 saying he looked suspicious. When three Aurora police officers arrived they threw him to the ground and forcibly restrained him with a carotid hold, while paramedics administered 500mg of ketamine, an extremely powerful sedative. Elijah went into cardiac arrest and three days later he was pronounced brain dead. On August 30th, 2019 Elijah was taken off life support. Elijah Mcclain was deeply loved, he was a son, a healer, a brother, an artist, and self taught violinist who played for stray kittens in shelters to keep them company. #JusticeForElijahMcClain

Original art by Tahla Tessier, **www.tessiearts.com**

Sean Monterrosa—Just one week after the murder of George Floyd, 23 year old Sean Monterrosa was murdered by police in Vallejo, CA. Sean was a brown artist who believed in protesting for Black and Brown lives and fighting against police brutality. Sean was shot 5 times and murdered after already surrendering and kneeling to police officers on June 2nd, 2020. Sean was an artist who worked with brown youth in the community and cared deeply for Justice for POC everywhere. He was known in life to be a loving son, brother, and friend. Poster by Dignidad Rebelde.

Through a week of revolutionary uprisings, state violence against black and brown communities has brutally escalated. **Erik Salgado** was 23 years old when he was publicly executed at the hands of police on June 6th, 2020 in East Oakland, CA . His pregnant girlfriend was also shot and survived. Unfortunately, due to the delay of emergency medical treatment, she lost their unborn child. According to neighbors accounts, Salgado drove onto their block and was boxed in by undercover police trucks. He then revved the engine and began spinning the tires, burning rubber. When the engine popped, two officers unloaded on him. Salgado was unarmed when three California highway Patrol officers (CHP) unloaded 40 rounds on him and his girlfriend. Those who knew and loved Erik will always remember him as a son, father, partner, and friend.

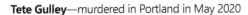

Tete Gulley—murdered in Portland in May 2020

In loving memory of all people lost to state violence of all kinds, including those whose names and faces we don't know.

Chapter 5
Poetry Journalism on Po'Lice Terror and Resistance

I hear voices, see faces, of people I killed...
PNN's We-Search on the Military Industrial Complex

A Poem for Papa Bear

an Unhoused Poverty Skola who resided outside at Van Ness
and Geary, San Francisco (Ohlone /Lisjan Village of Yelamu)

Tiny Gray-Garcia

A thumb is a terrible thing to waste
Black, poor and disabled thumbs legs and lives
are perceived as trash when u live outside
after all we are not human in your eyes
just an "unsightly" tribe—
lost our humanity & persona-alities on the curbs, inside of
    doorways
and on the road-side
Excuse me sir—do u have any spare change?
On hard cement working cement aisles of objectified hate—
standing on street corners, working cardboard and cups
maybe a blink of your eye gets us a sliver of your disgust-filled love
My Name is Papa Bear—did 3 tours in your empire wars—
killing people you never had to see ,think about or care for
Now I'm houseless in these stolen United Snakes streets

Right in front of your eyes
and yet i exist nowhere
the only people who see me
are people who hope i disappear
Receiving 260 citations and now jail because you see me as trash
because you called the Po'Lice instead of listened to my ask—
I died
I'm no longer there
only exist as a memory in your cluttered past
I was killed from the violence of your not wanting me here....

(see story on Papa Bear in the Po'Lice stories section of this book)

Exercise Your Right to Shoot

Junebug

Junebug: "I took this photo of the police detaining children in my neighborhood (the Fillmore). I was at the bus stop and had to witness this shit, made me even more appreciative that we have Deecolonize Academy. Break the pipeline to prison. Stop the killing of our children."

"SINCE YOU WANT TO EXERCISE YOUR RIGHT TO SHOOT, I WILL EXERCISE MY RIGHT TO SPEAK THA TRUTH..."

"FUCK THA POLICE"!

SIRENS LOUD
SOUNDS OF THA BEAST,
THA POLICE OFFICER,
THA WICKED OVERSEER.
IN 1993 KRS ONE PREACHED.
IN 1990 PUBLIC ENEMY TEACHED
"911 IS JOKING YO TOWN."

FROM THA KKK LYNCHING TO COPS SHOOTING
NOW THA PEOPLE LOOTING.
BLACK LIVES MATTER RECRUITING
SOLIDARITY IN SOCIETY.

SYSTEMATIC RACIZM ARE ACTS OF GENOCIDE AGAINST
BLACK LIVES.

LEARN THA HISTORY OF POLICE,
YOU LEARN SLAVE PATROL 1704
GUARD THA RICH AND CRIMINALIZE THA POOR.
KILL THE INDIGENOUS AND PROTECT THE RESIDENT
1838 BOSTON PROTECT PRIVATE PROPERTY AND NOT THE
    PEASANT

LISTEN TO BODY COUNT
THA WORDZ OF ICE T...
"NO LIVES MATTER."
CUZ COPS ARE CRIMINALS
THEY HARM US, NOT HELP US
WE MUST TAKE OUR SAFETY SERIOUSLY.

HAVING A FAMILY COUNCIL NOT CPS INVOLVED
WE MUST BE THE SOLUTIONS TO SOLVE
KEEP OUR CHILDREN OUT THA SYSTEM
RESIST THA CONDITIONING OF BROKEN LAW
AND NOT CALL.

"FUCK THE POLICE!"

Cop With PTSD? What!

Leroy F. Moore, Jr.

Chorus
Who shot you
Who shot you
Who shot
Who -n- a fuck shot you

Verse
Bringing back Ice Cube's Ghetto vet
In his wheelchair with a bullet proof vest
Popo rolled by
Flash back to that drive by

Chorus
Who shot you
Who shot you
Who shot
Who -n- a fuck shot you

Verse
It's like boyz n da Hood
Coronavirus, get back in the house
I wish I could, you gentrify
I'll stay on this porch so bye bye

Bridge
My wheelchair is the spirit of John Singleton
Pushing through these streets of compton
I know where I'm going
My roots ground me where I have been

Chorus
Who shot you
Who shot you
Who shot you
Who -n- a fuck shot you

Verse
It was you, The boys in Blue
Like the Ghetto Boys, your mind is playing tricks on you
Shouting at no one
That's no PTSD, you know you did wrong

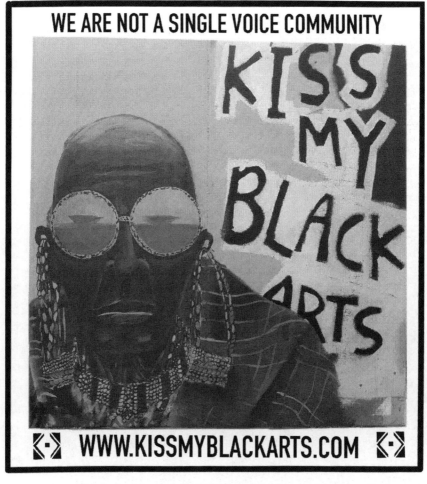

Original art by Rtystk of Kiss My Black Arts collective

Fire and Ice

Liliana Esparza

Photo credit: *El Paso Times*

Fire and Ice
Some say the world will end in fire,
Some say in Ice.
From what I've know
I hold with those who favor fire.
But if I had to perish twice.
I know enough to hate crime done by ICE
That for destruction of Humanity it definitely will be ICE.

Untitled

Equipto

We do what we can..
With what's in our hearts..
for our future generations.
For our ancestors.
For our families.
For what's right.
For what's left.
For those who can't.
For those who couldn't.
For our freedom.
For our people.
For Justice.
Forever.

#JusticeOrElse

El Tren De La Muerte

Teresa Molina

El tren buscando la muerte sin boleto ni documento empezando el viaje se avientan hacia los vagones nerviosos desesperados por el hambre y el desierto los detiene solo piensas en llegar al norte. En el camino se encuentran soldados policías—la migras golpes maltratos y los gritos "Perros mojados". Venimos rotos destruidos de nuestro país dejamos todo familia casa hijos para encontrar peor trato. Fin es nuestro destino.

The Train of Death

The train looking for death without a ticket or document, starting the journey they throw themselves towards the wagons nervous, desperate for hunger, and the desert stops them only if you think about reaching the north. On the way there are police soldiers—the migrants, beatings, mistreatment and the shouts "Wet dogs". We come from our country broken, destroyed, we leave all our families with children to find worse treatment. End is our destiny.

Untitled

Cat Brooks

Woke up with the weight of the world on my mind
Anxiety flowing through my body like electricity after being hit by
    lightning
for the second time
in as many days
as I can remember since the shit hit the fan
Again
And
I'm at a loss to describe the cost of the loss of the sanity of this
    country
Or maybe it's always been gone
But I've got a sinking feeling it won't be long before even the most
    cynical among us are
shocked at the cost of humanity that even Hannity will be moaning
Yes even on Fox News
Cause nobody knew
How bad this shit was gonna get

But what to expect
When we workshop hate and idolize greed
And America's morals come from TV
shows
with no basis in reality
Branded as reality shows
That show us how to be less than human
When little girls can't walk down the street and your President
    tweets hatred by the second
What can we expect when lynching is still legal as long as the body
    is Black and the
perpetrator blue
When folks with different views
can't even have a conversation
And most of my folks still languish on plantations
Oh wait—you call them prisons
Kept captive from their children
And you wanna talk about family values
But what value should little Black boys have for a country that sees
    them as invisible pawns
for profit they will never touch
Can't expect them to care too much
for lives they know they'll never fully live
Forgive
Forgive and forget
While continuing to let
white supremacy thrive which in the eyes of some is an expression
    of constitutional freedom
to bear arms and sing songs
about the good old days when Dixie reigned and niggers knew their
    place
Look me dead in my face
and tell me I should pledge allegiance to your flag that was too
    good to bury our dead
who died for this country you love so much
Your pride
can't touch
my rage as I watch America turn yet another page

of Hate
In the so-called land of the free where I can't even just be
an educated Black woman walking down the street
without fear
Fear of
Cops
Vigilantes
Racists
Rapists
And yes
Even my own kind
Who've been so wounded
That even I look like the enemy
Hurt people hurt people you see
This shit ain't a democracy
So stop talking to me
Like I am a child
Who somehow just doesn't understand how this shit really works
Knee jerk
Political Pundits Pontificate
on tv
manipulating the truth of what we see on cameras taken from
    soldiers on the front lines of
this latest war against the poor
And the Black
And our allies
Who are deemed enemies of the state
See
It's really you lovers of freedom that are the proponents of hate
And how dare you fight back
Or cry foul
Sit down
Shut up
Don't march
Don't scream
How dare you cry
Your only job
is to continue to choke on the lie

That is America
And pray that you can breathe
Can you?
Can you breathe?
Cause I can't
This knee in my neck has been there since before I took my first
     breath
I've spent a lifetime learning to inhale through my nose and dodge
     nooses camouflaged in
neo liberal talk about equality with no equity or any real desire for
     me to be an equal
Both the prequel and the sequel
to this nightmare are right there for you to see
but really seeing
Requires you to suspend your belief of anointed supremacy
that allows you to gain from
The pain and the blood and the shit that stain
That flag you love so much
This country you swear no other can touch
You really love America?
Then get off your ass and make her be the country you are
     screaming at me that she is
The land of the free?
For who?
You?
Is that enough?
I call your bluff
And dare you to do more
And I suggest you move soon
Cause consequences loom
And karma has gone from knocking to banging at the door

From the West Berkeley Shellmound to Moana Nui

Fuifuilupe Niumeitolu

The Desecration

The desecration of the Sacred, violence against her Native woman
    body
persistent upon his arrival.

he brought out all the instruments of progress
baptized and renamed her Berkeley
her body submerged under him,
he is heavy and unrelenting as Empire

her plaited black hair,
he wrangled into platitudes, singed the iridescent strands to silence
he is the weight of asphalt, a lonely parking lot,

his ownership of her, he terms as "freedom."

The Tongan Mormon Baptism Ceremony

I am an eight year old girl at my Mormon baptism Ceremony,
in a small chapel in Maʻufanga, Tonga,
my hair plaited and split in two, a division so inconsolable,
my mother tenderly tied the wounds with bright white ribbons to
    mark this moment, the missionaries termed as the "coming of
    the light."

under a leaning breadfruit tree outside the Mormon chapel
hungry dogs mate, irrespectively, of the piety inside

his priesthood authority intrusive like the bleached baptismal water
surrounds me, my black hair contorted in their nets,
severing the cycles of memories,
until I am no longer able to discern my breath from drowning.

he renames me, declaring the Moana on behalf of his Gods,

bounded my feet with ropes made from woven human hair, lined
　　with spears of whale bone tied with knotted fau, baptized and
　　converted me
into a carcass of an obedient daughter and wife.

This moment, he proudly records in his missionary diary as "light."

We Are Still Here

The West Berkeley Shellmound,
her Native woman body rests under asphalt, luminous mana
　　silenced by a parking lot, man-made and mundane,
she is their private property owned by a white settler family who
　　refuse to negotiate with Indians.

On the battle grounds in Huichin and in 'Uiha,
Under the hands of missionaries and mercenaries,
our childrens' bones hung from trees like decomposed fekika fruit
the flagrant sour taste on our tongues
when we thought all was lost,
the Sacred was there, she picked up our memories, ancestors left for
　　dead
she fed our mouths with the flesh of sweet acorn and salt water
　　from her breasts until we grew strong,
fearless,

she weaves the circuitous dance of death and birth into her long
　　black hair, dreamtimes exchanged through collective breaths,
　　from our Moananui to Huichin,
she coughs origin stories, birthed before his arrival, innumerable
　　constellations, they grow in our altars like the flowing yellow
　　pua garlands in our hair

she is survivor, creation, Creator
always here

yes, we remember, the stories of us after the missionary and
　　mercenary are gone.

Broken System

By Cyndi Mitchell

Mario Romero, a father, brother, and son who was murdered and attacked for being black, having both his hands up, and sitting in his own car in front of his own home on Sept. 2, 2012. His murderers are Sean Kenney and Dustin Joseph of Vallejo PD #Justice4MarioRomero

What is a human life worth?
Beaten in the street...body drug through the dirt

To protect and to serve...What does that really mean
Kill first then fake fear is all that's seen

If it's not a taser then it's a gun
Those paid to protect are torturing us and our loved ones for fun

To beat a man was not enough
Repeated murder is practiced to prove whose tough

How much is a human life worth?
A man is senselessly robbed of life on earth

To protect and serve communities and people Like
Mario Romero Guy Jarreau Oscar Grant Ernest Duenez and
    Rahiem brown

Yes the system has let them down.
To protect and serve Communities and people Like
Kenneth Harding, Jared Huey, little James Rivera, Andy Lopes,
    Idress Stelley and most recently Kelly Thomas

Yes the system and government has broken it's promise.

It's time for us to rise up against injustice ..case by case
expose each murderer face by face

we must make those in high positions give a damn
to prevent injustice like what was done to Rahmarley Graham

Take our marches out into the streets
then on to the front porches of those hiding behind the white
    sheets
Racism Classism Death or Prison
Are the only options freely given in a broken system

Untitled

Bella Martrice

I am the artist

Paint the perimeter
Of my body
Yielding yellows
I stretch halos
To protect my
Spirit from

Them boys
They, Deadly
My brother man man
and I was wondering
Why the police stopped us.

We was wondering what fuckin
Justification
Did they have to convince themselves we
We're criminals
I wonder what was that mutha fuckin
Officers
Internal dialogue
And
I a social doctor
Diagnosed
That mutha Fucka a racist
They had no reason to
Racially profile is and have all of their weapons drawn when we had
    not broken
The law

Why did they call every fuckin cop in the vicinity
Why were all of their guns drawn
Why are they so afraid of us

Brown and Black Bodies

Shell spirits
Have ancestors that whisper to trees
And know ancient. Secrets your history
Can't hear my God's voice
Our deceased are spiritual
Tour guides. We chant with babies
Unborn... Before they arrive
The officer yelled,
With a blood hungry lust in his voice
Anxious...…..... anxiously yelled
throw your keys out of the window....
Get out the vehicle with your hands up
20 mental
Health issue
having white supremacists boys in
Blued
Guns
Drawn

Don't turn around... He didn't allow for us to look at them

I have exited.
Autopilot
Hyper trauma
Safeguard activated

I'm
Triggered
They are trigger happy. .

My ex co-worker is screaming.
It's my turn,
To exit the car
This is yet another stage
Action .....
Do not turn around
The same blood curling voice
Repeated to me
Put your hands up.

Get
On
the

I follow instructions
Like a script written for me

This ain't no dress rehearsal.
I've been here before

It's action....

She has a weapon!!! An officer screamed

Action.

No, you do.

Their Shoes

Equipto

When ya living in Frisco,
& lied to by all these city officials.
Sometimes I wonder what it's gonna take for you to fight.
Just remember, housing is a human right.
Show respect for community.
Knowing we all just a check away from losing it. Following this
    blueprint with faith & hope it'll work,
like the Young Lords, taking over a church.
It's all blasphemy, this ain't the way that it has to be. Every shelter is
    filled to capacity.
See the bankers, the shiesters & creditors,
Opened the door for the corporate developers.
It brought emptiness, feeling like I'm love sick.
My friends homeless & homies I grew up with, are
Alone in the mind, no contact with family,
They're scarred for life, afraid of reality.
A survivor-not a casualty.
A human being-not a faculty. Let that sink in. Fall on some hard
    times. Maybe you'd think twice, What would it be like, in
    THEIR SHOES.

STOLEN

Christy Garcia

Dedicated to JV "Free Aztlan"

They can try to keep you caged but your spirt
and soul will always be consciously free

You take our babies marking them before they can walk
Child stained with
reflection, part of a problem.
Stolen from them the opportunity to do the internal work,
Years after the corrupted system repeatedly broke them down to the
    core of transparent cries for help
The trauma left behind
Stolen Brown Baby
Criminalized,
we will keep telling history through your oppressed eyes
And though you at 12 understood the life and disadvantage of
    having colored skin you stayed woke to the circumstances,
you shaped your mindset and were capable of change
No brother gets left behind
all hands on deck
boots to the ground
a brown brothers struggle for freedom at last finally found
20 years later once again you fall victim to systematic racism
Drapped from head to feet with their biased ass opinions
We resist,
Against those
who you speak with courage to denounce
Wrong place, wrong time
No chance to draw that line
Stolen was the day
Your freedom was denied
"Across the board"
Through the mouth of the beast himself
The beast
That your momma read to you about

in those stories written and carved upon her skin
Embedded into our bloodline before the concept of understanding,
the malinche of our present time taking and breaking our sangre
Across the board
Moments Stolen
From the streets where you were meant to informally mend and
    that line to bend
Stolen brown baby
Right from your momma arms
The struggle is real you've been marked
We Dont entertain,
We use our given skills to break that chain
No gavel,
No 12 nefarious souls,
No subsequent exploited badge
Stolen Baby you are...
but a mirrored image of years of hate
Stolen Baby you are....
but a mirrored image of years of unjust treatment
Stolen baby you are...
but a mirrored image that will be shattered of this systematic
    oppression
Stolen baby your struggle will continue on roads painted and
    tainted colored of brown freedom.
Stolen Baby....

Original art by Joey Villarreal created in the SHU "torture cell" at
Pelican Bay and from the book *Aztlan Realism* by Aztlan Press

Chapter 6

What We Can Do & Resources

Suggestions on Police Brutality Against People with Disabilities Beyond Training.....

Leroy F. Moore, Jr.

Mr. Musa Fudge, Black disabled man in SF abused by 14 cops with a title of the documentary film, *Where Is Hope: The Art of Murder Police Brutality & Disability*

Yes, I talk a lot about the problems so here are some of my suggestions toward police brutality against people with disabilities and who are Deaf.

SOME of My Suggestions: So what can we do as a community more locally?

1 Switching the focus from what the police needs to what the community needs.

2 Not saying that loved ones shouldn't sue. We have to realize that $$ is coming from us the taxpayers. Can you imagine if that $$$$$ came out of police's pockets? If we can get in touch with families that lost a disabled/Deaf member by police brutality and offer our support and disability justice advice.

3   Team up with Malcolm X Grassroots Center, other Black orgs/Black disabled activists to do reports, studies and papers on police brutality with Black/Brown disabled/Deaf people.

4   Continue to write about it especially in the Black media on Black twitter

5   Institutionally—recommend that our disability orgs take on the issue of police brutality against our youth and young adults by offering: community forums, training, art/music programs on the topic of state violence, workshops on how not to call 911.

6   Make inroads into NAACP about disability justice

7   Demand that anti-police brutality groups take a workshop on disability justice by @Sins Invalid, Patricia Berne, 'Never Call The Police Workshop by Poor Magazine, Lisa Tiny Gray-Garcia

8   Support local activists/orgs who are doing groundbreaking work in police brutality and disability/Deaf like the Idriss Stanley Foundation La Mesha Irizarry in SF, Center for Convivial Research and Autonomy, Annie Paradise and Advance Youth Leadership Power in Chicago, Candace Marie

9   Use tools that are already out there like: Where Is Hope film documentary, Emmitt Thrower and more

10   As you have seen that I didn't mention policy and police reform because it is all about community control.

11   Get to know your neighbor and their families and talk about how they can be more aware of disability in everyday and in a crisis situations, so you can call them, not the police.

12   Demand these big federal grants that go to national disabled orgs have real community buy in.

13   Work with others who are collecting data on this issue to make sure disabeled and Deaf people are not only included, but are a part of the researching team.

14   Look internationally on police brutality and disability and what people with disabilities are doing.

We can demand more non-grant money, media and awareness to go to cultural projects like Krip-Hop Nation, Poor Magazine and Sins Invalid, etc. who have a record doing cultural work around police brutality against people with disabilities and many others. We can support the National Black Disability Coalition, Jane Dunhamns' work around implementing Black Disability Studies, at colleges and universities and their work in the community creating advocacy and cultural outlets to Black families and Black disabled people. As street activists in this fight against police brutality can start and continue to ask the following: are our rallies accessible, is the disabled community represented not only in your rallies but on the stage, on your media, in your talking points and are the politics of disability justice practice implemented in social justice left and their work before and during a movement?"

People after my presentation on police brutality against people with disabilities ask, what about training; and says I'm too harsh when it comes to police training. My answer always have been if you want to continue down this road of police training, then people with disabilities need institutional power to write a national report and have the power to implement it. Anything else is a waste of time!

An example of Krip-Hop cultural work with a spin to it by @ Kounterclockwise aka Deacon Burns and Kaya Rogue video The Whip (**www.youtube.com/watch?v=XJ1leQVhaOE**).

10 (11 or 12) Things you can do to Not ever call the Po'Lice, CPS and APS

The beginning of a life-long list created by POOR Magazine/Prensa POBRE/Homefulness family)

Tiny Gray-Garcia

1 DegentriFUK (degentrify) Your Individuated Life—<u>If your family of origin is safe and has space, go home</u>. Explanation: If you have bought into the Away-Nation—cult of Independence as we call it at POOR Magazine—so rigorously drummed into your head from the time you leave the womb in kkkapitalist amerikkklan, and systems telling you to move away from your language, parents, community of origin, even if it is a safe and loving place, begin the long process to resist this capitalist notion of individalism and separation. (POOR Magazine offers PEopleSkool seminar on Decolonization and DegentriFUkation to help you with this). If your home, community/town of origin is not a safe place, work long and hard (and it's VERY hard) to build your circle of support with your chosen family.

2   Launch, Create, Work toward creating a Circle of Support—
    complete with a text/phone tree of phone numbers of friends,
    supporters, family members who agree to be called by each other
    in a case of an emergency. Expand on this to include community
    elders, spirit and prayer-bringers, advocates, lawyers, therapists
    and healers.

3   De-Racialize/De-kkkapitalize your world-view—Shake ALL as
    much of the white-supremacy notions of "clean" spaces defined
    by kkkorporate world-views of cleanliness" out of the deep
    recesses of yo mind—in other words if you see an unhoused
    person sitting on the sidewalk—on your street— please realize
    this isn't something to automatically pathologize, be scared of, or
    consider to be dangerous. Look into your heart and subconscious
    and think back to when you got that message. Similarly, if you
    are a non-black person of color, or white person, deconstruct
    your own tendencies to feel "unsafe" at the site of a Black or
    melanin-rich person.

4   Begin repeating a mantra—"Calling 911 doesn't mean help,
    support or safety" and replace it with "911 means possible death"
    and create a phone tree/ phone text list with your support networks
    of chosen family, friends, care-givers, people you trust who are
    willing/able to come through.

5   Research, become involved in groups like Critical Resistance,
    APTP and resources like Concern (mental health crisis) and
    other anti-police terror work.

6   kkkop-Watch ANYTIME you can—stand by and watch, report and
    call in as many people as possible whenever you see anyone being
    stopped, frisked, questioned, harassed by the paid murderers.

7   Teach your families, elders, communities about the myth of 911,
    de-racialization and decolonization, and the ideas you learned
    here today.

8   Un-fund Adult Protection Services/stop calling APS except when
    elder abuse by Eviction is happening. Take care of your elders
    and your community even if it takes time—capitalism and death
    and criminalization takes time.

9 Un-Fund Child Protection Services/stop calling CPS—Cuz it attacks poor families of color, and instead, educate yourself in the Transubstative error of cross-cultural differences—stop pathologizing poverty, houselessness and cultural differences. If you are a teacher, educator or counselor, work with restoration models instead of separation models.

10 Read How to Not Call the kkkops EVER article, come to next training offered by POOR Magazine on July 15, 2018 or invite us to your town, city, school or barrio (email us at **poormag@gmail.com** for more information) and check out the release of *POVERTY scholarship—A PeoplesTextBook— poor people-led theory, art, words and tears across mama earth*, available on **poorpress.net**.

11 Support POOR, indigenous and POC led movements like Sogorea Te Land Trust, Community Ready Corps, Homefulness, Idriss Stelly Foundation and education and support models outside of non-profit industrial complex models of "safety".

12 Support/become involved in mediation clinics like Berkeley's SEEDS and/or get trained in mediator skills.

13 Learn about Community Reparations, African Peoples and Indigenous Peoples Land reclamation and Reparation Movements and become an active reparations, land and hoarded resources redistribution (more about this from movements like Zapatistas in Chiapas, Shackdwellers Union in South Africa and Homefulness)

14 Call the Fire Department directly—they have their own phone numbers in every city in the US if you are looking for paramedic or other emergency services.

15 Call MHFirst—a powerFULL grassroots movement to support people Po'Lice free without EVER calling the kkkops—reach them at 510–999–9MH1 or MH1Oak on facebook, Instagram and Twitter

Resources:

- Black Disability Youth Coalition in Chicago
- Anti Police-Terror Project
- Community Ready Corps

- Peoples Community Medics
- Poor Peoples Security Team at POOR Magazine (**www.poormagazine.org**) @Poormagazine on IG, Fb & Twitter
- MH First

CAHOOTS

White Bird Clinic
Eugene | Springfield

DISCLAIMER: POOR Magazine does not affiliate with CAHOOTS because they engage with the police force. We are sharing this as a resource because this organization is an alternative to directly calling the Po'Lice.

Organization in Eugene, Oregon that works with police de-escalation training and provides medical services.

CAHOOTS (Crisis Assistance Helping Out on The Streets) provides mobile crisis intervention 24/7 in the Eugene-Springfield Metro area. CAHOOTS is dispatched through the Eugene police-fire-ambulance communications center, and within the Springfield urban growth boundary, dispatched through the Springfield non-emergency number. Each team consists of a medic (either a nurse or an EMT) & a crisis worker (who has at least several years' experience in the mental health field).

Any person who reports a crime in progress, violence, or a life-threatening emergency may receive a response from the police or emergency medical services instead of or in addition to CAHOOTS.

Community Crisis Hotline: Available 24/7. Call 541-687-4000 or toll free at 1-800-422-7558.

Email: Info@whitebirdclinic.org

Interview on Po' People's Revolutionary Radio—PNN KEXU 96.1FM—with Asantewaa from MH First

Anti Police-Terror Project

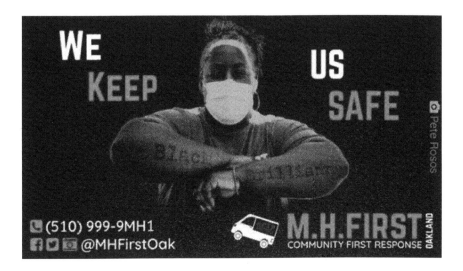

MH First is a program created by Anti Police-Terror Project and launched by APTP's Sacramento Chapter. MH First is a mobile mental health first responder team made up of doctors, nurses, organizers, mental health professionals, peers, and community members.

MH First provides mental health crisis response, domestic violence safety planning, and support and destigmatization for substance use disorder and mental health. Our three person team will use de-escalation techniques, non-punitive and life affirming interventions, safety planning, and accompaniment to provide community members with much needed services.

We are not a 501c3, we work on volunteer power. We are a community based program and not dependent on 911 nor police for participant contact.

> TINY: So as you know, a lot of us warriors in the fight against this po'lice terror across this occupied land

have been calling for the end of po'lice, the end of funding them, and the end of enabling them. Some of us hardcore warriors have been teaching-walking and never calling them, as you know many of us at POOR Magazine teach and speak on. We are blessed to have a powerful sister warrior in this fight and a revolutionary from Anti Police-Terror Project, who just was part of the launching of a powerful movement to enable us folk to rely on each other, which is called MH First, or Mental Health First. Welcome, Asantewaa to Poor People's Radio.

ASANTEWAA: Thank you. Thank you. It's a pleasure to be here.

TINY: Fasho. Can you tell listeners whatever you need to tell us about this powerful project you guys just launched?

ASANTEWAA: Sure. So one thing that I always like to mention, and I heard you touch on it when you were talking, that some of us are committed to not calling the police, right? And one of the things about that is it forces us to be creative and undo some of that conditioning, right? So MH First existed organically in our own community because some of those same commitments, but when some of our comrades or family or friends were having these similar crises, we really just dealt with them. Whether it was making schedules, or making meals, or literally sitting on folks, or you know, talking folks to appointments, or you know, whatever it is we had to do, we just did it to keep our folks well, and we began to ask ourselves, why couldn't we make this available to the larger community, right? So when we started MH First in Sacramento, it was this group of folks that some folks have medical experience, some folks didn't, but most importantly, we really wanted to listen to folks that had had those adverse experiences while in a mental health crisis with police. And that is what really informed the way that we created the program. So,

we launched in January of 2020, and we partnered
with a clinic here in Sac. Also another establishment,
Harm Reduction Services, gave us a vehicle,
and we were legit up and running, and we were
crowdsourcing our original funds that we used to get
up, which was enough to purchase a cell phone and
survival supplies, right, for folks that are unhoused.
Because one, we understood that a great deal of calls
was going to be those "Oh, there's someone who's
unhoused and maybe they're behaving erratically",
so we were really intentional about making sure that
we built into our program outreach so that when
we're not on calls, we're out in the street talking to
folks, giving folks supplies, and making sure people
have blankets, and if folks are using substances,
making sure that if they are using, that they're using
as safely as possible. We wanted to make sure to
incorporate that because there is prevention work,
right, that we could be doing outside of just reacting
when someone is in a crisis, and then also just the
opportunity to build relationships with folks that are
in the community so they know to call us instead
of calling the police. When we started, we had this
really long list of things that we wanted, right? Like,
the sky was the limit, money wasn't a thing, like,
what kind of program would we build? So, that is
our inspiration, right? A 24-hour respite center;
wraparound psychiatric services; absolutely from the
top to the bottom, no police involvement. And even
de-medicalizing how we interact with folks around
their mental health and creating a framework that is
really self determined, right? Not, we swoop in and
we tell you when you're okay, or we're like "just be
normal" kinda shit. Like really meeting folks where
they're at and letting them determine what is safe
for them, letting them determine what is healthy for
them, and us just aiding them in getting to that thing.
In the midst, as the calls for defunding the police

became popularized in recent history, because, Tiny, as you know, we've been talking about defunding the police since before Oscar Grant, right?

TINY: Right! Thank you.

ASANTEWAA: Because they're stealing the money out our pockets, you know what I mean? But recently, the term has become popularized and a lot of folks now understand that one of the sectors that police can be essentially organized out of is mental health crisis response, right? Because we know that a lot of the times when police do kill or harm somebody, it's usually someone who's in the midst of a mental health crisis, and they don't have the training or the desire to do that work, right? And that's what's really at the bottom of the crisis, when we talk about police terror and mental health— these pigs don't want to do this work. They're not trained to do that work. And it shows in the way that they go about doing that work because they harm people, right? Their job is to incarcerate, apprehend, right, after crimes have been committed and not before. So when they're dealing with mental health crises, they're treating, essentially, our community members like criminals, like being sick is a crime. You know what I mean? And it shows, right, in the statistics. So, once that term became popularized, that people understood that that was the easy go-to on behalf of the establishment, who felt like they could just throw some money at something and put a bandaid to fix it, right? So there's all these interests from all over, of how do we do this, how do we do this, how do we do this? And there's not a lot of models that exist. But one of the side effects is that we've been able to replicate in Oakland already, starting on 8/28.

TINY: Whoop!

ASANTEWAA: We had our first weekend. They're available, Fridays and Saturdays from 8pm to 8am, and their telephone number is 510-999-9MH1. As Anti Police-Terror Project, we are super proud that we were able to take this thing that we did organically and make it available for the community, and we hope that as time goes by, that not just these 501(c)(3) funded type of programs, right? We wanna focus on folks to just be like, how do me and 5 people get together and figure this out? Like, how do we create our own system, and how do we create a system per block, or per square block, right, that is built and equipped and handle folk who are in the midst of mental health crisis in a way that is humane, in a way that is not criminalized, and in a way that is self determined by that person, right? Because we really have to start understanding mental health issues differently and understand how changing our environment is going to affect how folks are coping mentally, too. Like we don't really take that into account. We live in a capitalist system with nuclear families, right, which are built on keeping the folk under stress, right, which causes depression, which causes anxiety, right? And so I think as we begin to build another world and build other systems, we'll also see some shifts in how mental health issues show up in our communities, and even more so how we deal with them.

TINY: Right. Beautiful work, beautiful palabras. So this is deep on so many levels. You probably know, we've been teaching in these "How to Not Call the Po'Lice Ever" workshops since the absolute genocidal murder of so many of our young daughters and suns. Shout out to Mario Woods. Shout out to Luis Demetrio Gongora Pat. Just recently, Steven Taylor and so many more. It's absolutely mind numbing. And the piece around it, though is always, "what if I see someone having a mental health crisis? What should I do?" Well, first off, one of the things I love about what y'all are doing and what you're visioning and said is just that way of how do we help folks in the way they want to be helped? This is what I call the cult of rehabilitation in AmeriKKKlan, where we gotta fix everything that we see. Maybe nobody want no damn help, hello! I say that if they didn't have the violence of exposure, you wouldn't even know they were in crisis, right? But now you suddenly gonna "fix it" with a person with a gun. No! So I love that in that way, you're coming to that space, to that person, to that human, wherever they're at. Maybe they just want a blanket, right? Maybe they want to be left alone, like a lot of us when we get depressed, hello? That part. I'm just wondering though, because I'm sure you've heard it, cuz you do the same work, and you're walking the same journey, that whole aspect of "well, what about if my female or male identified body is being violated", right? That always comes up. And I'm wondering how if at all, because this isn't, you know, that first, it's MH First. I'm wondering though, how do you see or how does that land on you?

ASANTEWAA: Man, that is like, yeah, there's certain questions that come up. Like, "well what about domestic violence" or "what about if someone has a gun" and "what if…?" all these things. And I think Cat has said something around this abolitionist theory, because you know, these are some of the same questions that come up, right? Like when we're talking about abolition and doing away with prisons, you know, there's lots of questions, like "what do we do with the rapists?" and "what do we do with the murderers?", you know? And I don't think we have to start answering that question there, as Cat says, right? Like, we could really look at the reality of it, and start answering the questions like "what do we do with folks that are using drugs?" Right? "What do

252

we do with folks that have trauma and expressing that trauma in a way that's really public or 'abnormal' " right? Because I don't have an answer for that. I don't. And I feel like a lot of us should get more comfortable with saying "I don't know". You know what I mean?

TINY: Right. (laughs) Exactly!

ASANTEWAA: Because that's what puts you in a place to honestly figure it out instead of just filling in the blank with something that sounds good.

TINY: Mm. Exactly. Exactly.

ASANTEWAA: So, I don't know. We haven't really run across it yet. I think that when we do, we'll have to ask ourselves some hard questions and do the best that we can, and if we make a mistake, we gotta learn from it and pray that we prevented some harm and don't cause any.

TINY: Asè. And another piece, I'm loving also, just I'm sure you've the only model that's ever talked about, which is cahoots, in the Pacific Northwest, in, what we have a problem with is they still f with the po'lice, right? So that ain't a solution to us, even though it's kinda more user friendly, and at least they're trying, but, no! I don't wanna have it. I love that you said "No, there's absolutely no engagement!" That's how we get down, right? Because no, we don't want to have "friendly relationship" navigating people with weaponry and tanks. That's not an option, right? But what I also wonder, too, just in your process of this, of building, of building this and building Oakland movement, and I'm gonna have you repeat that number again for listeners. I know that you did a training. We had to bus in and have some of y'all at Homefulness doing a training right here on this sacred land. Is there, it could be a ground swell that's pretty large, because what we just heard in Frisco is there's something like 50,000, put that number in our mouth, 50,000 well checks a day to po'lice. Like anybody should be calling them for a well check, hello?

ASANTEWAA: Oh my gosh.

TINY: That won't end up with you being well. Rest assured, shout out to sister Kayla Moore, ibaye. But I'm just wondering in terms of the ground swell, and as it grows, are you looking at having more trainings in the future? Are you looking at building? What's your thought on that?

ASANTEWAA: Yes, we are. We actually had, I think we had a conversation with San Francisco of what would it look like to train folks, non-police officers, in our model, like what would it look like to launch something like that, where we wanna train, actually, everybody we can, not just...of course if you do the training, it does qualify you to be a volunteer for MH First, but in no means does that mean that you have to be a volunteer for MH First. We really just want folks to have the information because part of the training is familiarizing folks what to look for: when's the right time to intervene, what type of intervention should be done, right? It really works on the interpersonal level and it also works on the level of, and when I say interpersonal, I mean dealing with family, friends, comrades, right? And then also, if you're in that position of a responder, it's not our goal just to train people who are going to be in MH First. We wanna train everybody as much as possible because we just wanna give them the tools that they need to mitigate these crises. Not just about the police, but the right way, without us.

TINY: Right. Thank you.

ASANTEWAA: You know what I mean? Like being able to do it without us. We want you to call us when you don't have no other choice, right? We can equip you with

254

the tools you need to mitigate the crisis on your own and that's dope.

TINY: That's what's up. Beautiful work. Beautiful spirit. Beautiful vision. What is the number again for MH First in Oakland?

ASANTEWAA: In Oakland, it is 510-999-9MH1.

TINY: And then Sac?

ASANTEWAA: And then we also take by DMs, you know the younger folks feel more comfortable typing, right? So it's MHFirstOak on all the platforms. And then for folks that are in the Sacramento area, our number is 916-670-4062. And we are MHFirstSac across all the social media platforms.

TINY: Asè, and we're gonna be putting this beautiful solution in the upcoming "How to Not Call the Po'Lice Ever Handbook". So much love. Alright, sis, we'll talk to you soon. Thank you.

ASANTEWAA: Thank you, Tiny.

Land Liberation/Un-Selling and Freedom from Po'Lice State Made Possible with ComeUnity Reparations

POOR Magazine Solidarity Family (folks with race, class, and/or formal education privileges)

Community Reparations, a concept launched by Lisa "Tiny" Gray-Garcia, is rooted in the notion of Interdependence. It's meant to be a healing medicine of resistance to the lie of independence and the separation nation, which encourages the violent act of looking away from people who are poor or unhoused.

Community Reparations instructs us all to resist capitalism's normalizing of separateness and "success" through land-stealing and wealth-hoarding.

Instead, Community Reparations recognizes our shared humanity and invites those of us who benefit from stolen or hoarded resources to engage in loving, radical redistribution of these resources.

What does reparations mean to you? Voices from POOR Magazine Solidarity Fam

"Doing the learning/unlearning work to understand how resource and land acquisition has been maintained culturally/ideologically as well as politically… Giving back and building relationships of support… Being a part of community and interdependence building and learning."

—Julian

"Reparations is active and is meant to help mend past/present/future wounds. It's a responsibility to the interdependence of earth and her residents. It's also seeing that my privilege has been precisely in being able to look away/disconnecting, and so reparations looks like having the hard conversations with family members about this stuff, and not avoiding."

—Miyuki

"I've always tried to be generous with sharing my resources. I haven't had a lot of money in the last 4-5 years. I do things like cook for people and drive people places. Reparations looks like mama giving money or other donations to churches and charities. Her way of showing gratitude for the abundance she has."

—Sandra

"Reparations are a way to heal and to repair broken connections and relationships with those who have been harmed by racism, capitalism, violence, and resource extraction. Reparations have deepened my relationships, and also make it clear that not all indigenous people left the area. This process has led to the formation of some of my closest relationships."

—Cynthia

"Naming the harm that I've caused or benefit from, doing what I can to respond to that harm with material resources that mitigate it."

—Jessica

"When we minimize the impact of slavery or of Native genocide or of the Chinese Exclusion Act or any other example of racism and oppression—we are lying. If your reaction to systems of oppression that you materially benefit from is anything other than wanting—truly wanting—to redistribute resources to mitigate that oppression—then you are lying to yourself about reality, and you will never get a chance to admit that you are human, or experience your own humanity. Reparations are the gateway from lies to life."

—Toby

"Reparations is a process of building relationships and connections to redistribute all kinds of access, knowledge, and skills in addition to financial resources. Reparations is what happens when folks with privilege use it to undermine the systems that exclude people in the first place. It comes from a place of compassion and responsibility, not guilt. It is doing what needs to be done because it is the right thing to do."

—A.S.

"Reparations means making up for past wrongs that my family, ancestors, and I have financially benefited from. It means that every dollar that sits in my bank account and every dollar that I spend is a dollar that cannot be accessed by folks of color. It means that I cannot be whole while I have access to wealth and others do not. Reparations are an opportunity for me to get free."

—Paige

Community Reparations Funds

The Bank of Community Reparations is a national fund of redistributed and stolen wealth that is distributed equally among poor and indigenous people-led land use projects. Resources redistributed to the Bank of Community Reparations may be designated to these specific funds:

Po' Mamaz Reparations Fund   Dedicated to redistributing resources directly to poor, unhoused and formerly unhoused single mamaz, (fathers) and children who are unable to afford rent, a drivable vehicle, diapers, food, and other emergency needs related to their survival and thrival.

Tech Reparations Fund   Dedicated to building/preserving the equity of poor and working class communities who have been displaced or are at risk of displacement due to the presence of Tech industries and their employees.

Homefulness Community Reparations Fund   Dedicated to building, launching and growing homefulness commUNITIES across Mama Earth. Homefulness is a self-determined landless people's solution to the housing crisis, and POOR Magazine is currently in the process of constructing a multi-unit housing complex in East Oakland to provide housing for houseless families. POOR Magazine is also preparing to launch Homefulness 2 in Chico/Butte County, the site of recent serious fires.

Radical Redistribution   Dedicated to emergency needs of Po' folks—not related to a specific fund but rather the need of traditionally silenced, criminalized communities in struggle.

To be a part of this crucial act of humanity visit **http://poormagazine. org/rev_donor**.

For more information on Revolutionary Giving to the Bank of Reparations, call (510) 435-7500 or email **poormag@gmail.com**. To register for the next PeopleSkool Seminar in Black August for Folks with Race/Class Privilege, or set up a set up a training, presentation, talk or individual conversation at your workplace, organization, or community email **deeandtiny@gmail.com** or go online to **www. racepovertymediajustice.org** or **www.poormagazine.org**.

Original art celebrating the launch of the Bank of
ComeUnity Reparations by A.S. Ikeda

A Demand from a Coalition of Houseless/Migrante/Indigenous/Poor and Disabled to Disband All Po'Lice Agencies Across Occupied Turtle Island and Fund People-led solutions.

POOR Magazine/Homefulness Family on a Stolen
Land Tour along BlackArthur Blvd

Since the Beginning of the original theft of Turtle Island, the subsequent colonial genocide waged against the 1st Peoples of this land, the enslavement and genocide of Black Peoples from the continent, militarizing and creation of false kolonial borders, colonial wars across Mama Earth, the criminalization and policing of public land and unhoused people in public Police and armies have been used to destroy, kill, terrorize and maim.

This humble demand to disband All Po'Lice Agencies Across Occupied Turtle Island is because we as houseless, migrant, indigenous, disabled, Black and Brown communities have felt this first-hand and have witnessed, experienced and suffered from ongoing State Sponsored Murder, harassment, sweeps, evictions, violence , deportations, exploitations, seizures and brutality of our families, communities and bodies.

In addition, this community of multi-racial, multi-ligual, multi-cultural, multi-spirited, disabled poor people building a homeless peoples self-determined land liberation movement that NEVER engages with the systems of PoLicing or other Governmental institutions that test, arrest, deport or incarcerate us, hereby declare that we continue to refuse and resist all state-sponsored murder, control, terror and curfews on this stolen land.

We do with the understanding that other community accountability models such as the Elephant circle at Homefulness and Community Ready Corps have been supporting communities for years without ever engaging with police or military agencies to solve our problems.

We are humbly demanding that the billions of dollars used to fund police are re-directed to liberate, purchase and free up land and resources to build poor people-led solutions to homelessness, education, healthcare and trauma such as Homefulness, radical redisribution, self-determined models such as HomiesEmpowerment and the Bank of ComeUnityReparations, Black led models such as the Black New Deal and land healing and indigenous land reclamation projects such as Sogorea Te Land Trust .

In Addition we lift up the lives and spirits of Breonna Taylor, George Floyd, Stephen Taylor, Tony McDade, Sean Monterosa & so many more who most recently sparked people to refuse, to resist and to Say NOT ANOTHER DEATH.

It is with prayer and humility, love and respect for all of us and especially the next seven generations that we release this demand.

Signed By

POOR Magazine/Homefulness/DeeColonize Academy
Krip Hop Nation
Indian People Organziing For Change (IPOC)
National Brown Berets Oakland
Self-Help Hunger Program
Lisa Ganser/PoorNewsNetwork Washington

Kim DeOcampo, Executive Director Angel Heart, Secretary
& Public Relations Officer; on behalf of Sacred Sites
Protection and Rights of Indigenous Tribes (SSPRIT)
Samsarah Morgan
Oakland Better Birth Foundation
South Asians for Black Lives
Asians4BlackLives
Creating Freedom Movements
India Currents
IdleNoMoreSF
(Others TBA)

A.S. Ikeda is a radical redistributor with POOR Magazine's Solidarity Family. They are an artist, book/graphic designer, and editor. See more of their work at **asikeda.com**

Made in the USA
Columbia, SC
23 October 2020

23308922R00146